CHALLENGES
A Process Approach
To Academic English

CHALLENGES

A Process Approach To Academic English

H. Douglas Brown
Deborah S. Cohen
Jennifer O'Day

Department of English
San Francisco State University

PRENTICE HALL REGENTS
Upper Saddle River, New Jersey 07458

Library of Congress Cataloging-in-Publication Data

Brown, H. Douglas, (date)
 Challenges : a process approach to academic English / H. Douglas
Brown, Deborah S. Cohen, Jennifer O'Day.
  p. cm.
 Includes index.
 ISBN 0-13-009085-9
 1. College readers. 2. English language—Composition and
exercises. I. Cohen, Deborah S., (date). II. O'Day, Jennifer,
(date). III. Title.
PE1417.B724 1991
808'.042—dc20   90-40084
                                         CIP

Editorial/production supervision
and interior design: **Shirley Hinkamp**
Cover design: **Bruce Kenselaar**
Pre press buyer: **Ray Keating**
Manufacturing buyer: **Lori Bulwin**
Photo research: **Page Poore**

© 1991 by Prentice Hall Regents
Prentice-Hall, Inc.
A Simon & Schuster Company
Upper Saddle River, NJ 07458

Printed in the United States of America
10

ISBN 0-13-009085-9

Prentice-Hall International (UK) Limited, *London*
Prentice-Hall of Australia Pty. Limited, *Sydney*
Prentice-Hall Canada Inc., *Toronto*
Prentice-Hall Hispanoamericana, S.A., *Mexico*
Prentice-Hall of India Private Limited, *New Delhi*
Prentice-Hall of Japan, Inc., *Tokyo*
Simon & Schuster Asia Pte. Ltd., *Singapore*
Editora Prentice-Hall do Brasil, Ltda., *Rio de Janeiro*

CONTENTS

INTRODUCTION TO THE TEACHER

As we speed along through the last decade of the twentieth century, our attention is frequently drawn to enormous changes across the globe. Technology is advancing so rapidly that we can hardly keep up with all the developments. Scientific fields are creating better and better means for understanding and analyzing our world and the universe beyond. In the behavioral sciences we are discovering new ways of comprehending the complexity of dealing with ourselves, our companions, and our fellow human beings around the world. These changes present to all of us tremendous *challenges*. We are challenged to understand our environment, to utilize our resources, to take better care of our minds and bodies, and to work together as a human race for the good of all.

These global challenges are the subject matter of *Challenges: A Process Approach to Academic English*. The book is intended for students who are either already in, or will soon find themselves in, a university course of study in which English is the medium of instruction. As students of English as a foreign language focus on intrinsically interesting and relevant content, they are given means for effectively refining their language skills, especially skills of reading and writing.

The approach taken in this book is one in which reading and writing are seen as interacting linguistic forces through which students will develop their overall academic proficiency. Students are guided through numerous reading strategies that extract information from the printed page and then, through a process writing approach, they are shown that the act of writing itself helps to create, develop, and refine thinking processes.

Challenges may be described as a content-centered approach to English language mastery. Students get caught up in real challenges that they are facing in their own lives and, in many instances, in their own academic fields of interest. Therefore, from the outset the book does not so much tell them what they should be interested in, but rather it gives them further information about what already interests them.

To that end, this book encourages a learner-centered or cooperative approach in which students are encouraged to be creative in their ideas and outlook. Reading research has shown that understanding the written word involves the reader's bringing background information *to* a passage as well as discerning an author's intended meaning. In *Challenges*, a reading passage will have an intended purpose or message, but students are stimulated to derive their own messages by bringing their own perspectives to bear on the readings and to draw their own conclusions. Readings are not presented with the assumption that only one interpretation is valid; rather, many interpretations are encouraged as the creative mind of the student interacts with the readings.

Similarly, writing is not the act of planning everything you want to communicate ahead of time and then putting it on paper. Writing is a means for thinking, a method of developing ideas and of fleshing out arguments. Recent research in writing suggests that students write more freely and creatively when their writing emerges gradually from a number of sources of insight such as reading material, class discussions, and a teacher's individual attention. This book stimulates students to write on topics of intrinsic interest, to write a series of drafts, to get feedback on their writing from peers and teachers, and only then to consider that they have a "finished product."

The material in *Challenges* grows out of the collective experience of the authors in teaching courses in academic reading and writing. Some of the wisdom of our many years of classroom teaching experience is found in the accompanying *Teacher's Guide*. It consists of carefully designed sets of practical classroom activities for each of the segments of the ten units of the book.

We strongly encourage you to make use of the *Teacher's Guide*. The guide is especially useful for those who have not previously used certain methods that are used in *Challenges*. If, for example, you have not had an opportunity to have students do "clustering" as a rubric for organizing an essay, the *Teacher's Guide* carefully spells out how you might structure such an activity in the classroom. We also designed the guide to provide experienced teachers with some additional activities and ideas.

We wish you well as you embark on the adventure of joining your students in creatively exploring some of the pressing current challenges that will affect our future. As your students improve their academic English skills, they themselves will become better equipped to be shapers of tomorrow's world.

H. Douglas Brown
Deborah S. Cohen
Jennifer O'Day

San Francisco, May, 1990

CHALLENGES
A Process Approach
To Academic English

UNIT ONE

THE EVOLVING WORKPLACE: SOCIOLOGY

Western society for the past 300 years has been caught up in a firestorm of change. Change sweeps through the highly industrialized countries with waves of ever accelerating speed and unprecedented force.

Alvin Toffler in *Future Shock*

LESSON 1

FUTURE SHOCK

Human beings today are living in a world that has changed more in the past three decades than it had in the preceding three centuries. In the 1950s we suddenly entered the Space Age. Since then air travel and telecommunications have drawn together nations once distanced by great oceans. At the flick of a switch or the turn of a dial we can watch what is happening at this moment on the other side of the globe. Babies are being conceived in test tubes. Computers are learning to understand the spoken word. In this world, the latest technologies become obsolete overnight. Today the future is no longer predictable, so we must learn to adjust to a world that no longer resembles the one our parents knew or the one we expected to live in. We have only recently begun to understand how our rapidly changing globe constantly affects not only what we are doing but also what we plan to do. We are now learning that we must often ask ourselves, "Is our plan for tomorrow going to fit into the reality of the future?"

As a student in today's world, you will surely agree that this question is very important. Certainly, most of you are studying with the future in mind. Perhaps you are basing many of your decisions about your education on predictions about the job market of the future. Those of you already working in your chosen fields know that your occupations have undergone changes, often dramatic ones, in the last few years. When you think about the coming years, you might wonder if what you expect your occupation to be like is really the way it is going to be. Are you preparing now for what will become a reality or a dream? This question takes on an even greater significance when we consider one simple, but meaningful, statement: We will live the rest of our lives in the future.

Generating Ideas

● Brainstorming

Let's think about the future for a moment. Let's focus our attention on how it might affect your present or future job. Have you thought about the changes that might occur in your field? To help you think about this question, you are going to make two lists of ideas concerning changes in your field or in the field you plan to enter.

DIRECTIONS: Use your knowledge and imagination to follow these steps.

1. Prepare two sheets of paper with the following:
    a. What changes have occurred in my field in the last twenty years?
                    Your field—Today's Date
    b. What changes do I expect to occur in my field in the next twenty years?
                    Your field—the date twenty years from now
2. As quickly as possible, think of as many ideas as you can to answer the question on sheet a.
    a. Take between five and ten minutes to list every idea that comes to your mind.
    b. Do not evaluate your ideas. That will come later.
3. When you have written down everything you can think of, go over the list to evaluate what you have written. Cross out the ideas that don't fit.
4. Repeat this process (steps 2 and 3) for sheet b.

This process, called **brainstorming**, is a useful technique in writing because it permits you to approach a topic with an open mind. Because you do not judge your ideas as they emerge, you free yourself to come up with ideas that you might not even know you had. Brainstorming is one of several different ways to begin writing. In the following pages, we will introduce some other methods that will help you to explore ideas that you might want to write about.

● Working in a Group

In the preceding exercise you worked individually, using brainstorming to establish your own ideas, to follow your own train of thought. Another effective way to generate ideas is to work in a small group where you share your brainstormed ideas with the rest of the group members. By doing this, each of you will have an opportunity to further expand your own ideas.

DIRECTIONS: Form a small group (three to five people). Use the following guidelines for your group discussion.

1. Take turns reading your lists of changes in your field to each other.

2. Compare your classmates' lists to yours, looking for similarities and differences.
   a. Mark the changes on your list that are similar.
   b. Add to your list new ideas of changes that apply to your field.
3. As a group, select three changes that applied to the fields of each group member. If you have time, you can discuss these three ideas.
4. Choose a reporter from your group to share your three changes with the rest of the class.

Here is an example of what the compared lists of a group of three students might look like. (Notice that each list has some ideas that have been crossed out. These ideas had already been eliminated by the student in the last step of the brainstorming exercise because they did not fit.) The changes that were similar in each list have been labeled.

Teaching—Today	Sales—Today	Health Care—Today
attitudes toward teachers (A)	computerized inventory (D)	malpractice suits
information explosion (B)	customers' bad attitudes (A)	less respect (A)
union activity	distance from owners	hours
more job security	pressure	pay
better benefits (C)	meeting people	educational demands
use of textbooks	incentive pay	pressure
larger class size	consumer action	information increase (B)
computers as teaching tools	need to know more about products (B)	consulting with others
computers for record keeping (D)	more responsibility	competition for clients
competition for jobs	more advancement changes	advertising
greater student maturity	fewer personnel	computerized business (D)
higher diplomas	time clocks	computerized diagnosis
students' increased knowledge	less pay	greater benefits (C)
	better benefits (C)	

● Freewriting

You have just begun to explore the question of changes in your field. Some of your ideas will interest you more than others. Now you will have an opportunity to develop your thinking about one of these ideas.

DIRECTIONS: Follow these steps to generate further ideas on this topic.

1. From your lists of changes, choose one idea that interested you.
2. Write that idea at the top of a clean sheet of paper.
3. For ten minutes, write about this topic *without stopping*. This means that you should be writing something constantly.
   a. Write down everything that comes to your mind.
   b. Do not judge your ideas.
   c. Do not worry about your spelling and grammar.
   d. If you run out of things to say, continue writing whatever comes to your mind.

This process is called **freewriting**. It is designed to help you free ideas that you might not realize that you have. An important aspect of freewriting is that you write without being concerned about spelling, punctuation, or grammar. Of course, these elements of writing are important, but students' concern about them can sometimes inhibit the free flow of their ideas. Freewriting is a technique to generate ideas; it should be used as a beginning, as an initial exploration of the ideas that you have about a topic.

You can use your freewriting to help you get started with related writing tasks. In fact, you might want to refer to this freewriting when you are doing other writing tasks later in this unit. Therefore, you should put this and all other freewriting that you do into a notebook that you can refer to when you are generating ideas for future assignments.

LESSON 2

OUR FUTURE STOCK

About the Selection:

In the first lesson you had an opportunity to explore some of your thoughts about change and about the future of your field or occupation. Now you will have a chance to compare your predictions for the future with those of experts who have studied these issues in depth. The following reading selection is from the popular science magazine *Omni*. In 1982 the editors of *Omni* gathered information from various U.S. government agencies and industry experts. They used this information to develop a picture of what the work force and the economy of the future may look like. This selection is an excerpt from the article reporting their predictions. As you read through it, consider whether the changes mentioned here are similar to those you wrote about in lesson 1.

The First Reading

Before You Read: Anticipating the Topic

Look at the title and graphics. *Stock* often refers to an investment or an accumulation of something for future use. Judging from the subtitles and the pictures, what do you

think *stock* refers to in this case? _____

What type of future developments does this excerpt seem to focus on?

Based on the results of your brainstorming in lesson 1, write two to three sentences about the kinds of careers and workplace changes one could "put stock in" (expect; have faith in) for the future.

As You Read: Looking for the General Ideas

First read the article quickly to discover its main points and general organization. Then do the activities that follow. Later, in your second reading, you can go through the entire article more carefully or focus in on particular sections to pick up the specific details and development of the main points. You will see that two or three quick, purposeful readings will be more efficient and productive than one slow, detailed reading.

Don't worry about vocabulary! As you read, you will find words you do not know. Don't worry about these. Either guess their meanings or skip them entirely. *Do not* look up any words in the dictionary at this time. To do so would only slow you down and prevent you from focusing on the key points. Vocabulary exercises will follow.

OUR FUTURE STOCK:
A Survey of Jobs, New Technology, and the World Economy in the Next Millenium

1   During the next 50 years an incredible array of new technologies is expected to move from the lab to the world of business. We are already seeing evidence of this today. Robots are replacing humans on the production lines. Microcomputers have become fixtures in offices. Biofactories are beginning to manufacture batches of engineered human insulin.... The coming decades promise to be especially volatile[1] and exciting for American business. The expected upheaval will profoundly change not only our lives but also those of our children and grandchildren.

2   For the more developed nations, this era of turmoil will be marked by economic difficulties, problems with waste and pollution, and continually dwindling[2] resources. By contrast, the Third World countries will spearhead a new industrial age with the same fervor and energy that characterized American industrial expansion in the days of Vanderbilt, Carnegie, Morgan and Rockefeller...

[1]**volatile:** changeable
[2]**dwindling:** becoming smaller and smaller (in amount)

Courtesy of Chrysler Corporation

Job Markets and Careers

3   The technological revolution that will prevail[3] for the remainder of this century will create jobs and professions that as little as five years ago were nonexistent. These newly developed markets will demand of workers an understanding of sophisticated technical communications systems as well as an increased technical expertise. By the year 2001 basic skills that once were vital to

business will be rendered obsolete. The spot welder on the automobile production line, the clerk typist in an office, the field worker on a farm will go the way of the steamboat pilot and the blacksmith.

4   The most significant trend in years to come will be the shift from formation-type jobs (factory work, office typing, and general clerical work) to information-type jobs (programming, word processing, and supervising technical machinery).[4] The American economy will witness the demise

[3]**prevail:** occur as the most important feature

[4]**formation-type jobs:** jobs which result in the actual "formation" of a material product, such as a car, a manually typed report, and so on.

information-type jobs: jobs which focus on the electronic processing of information, whether that information is used in an office or business setting or used to control machines which then produce material goods and services. Note that this information may never take concrete material form; it can be processed and stored electronically in our computer systems, transmitted from one place to another by complex electronic telecommunications systems, and read on a computer screen rather than on separate sheets of paper.

Courtesy of IBM

of the blue-collar worker as automation and robotics become more prevalent, heralding the rise of the steel-collar worker. Such traditional blue-collar employers as General Motors and U.S. Steel have already begun to automate their factories—a fact reflected in the swollen[5] unemployment rolls in our industrial states.

5   By contrast, office and service jobs will be abundant, but only for those prepared to improve their technical skills. Again it will be automation that will displace many of the low-skilled and semiskilled workers in the present economy.

6   In fact, the era of the paperless office has already begun. It has been promoted by two principal developments: computers that process business information and the explosive growth of telecommunications systems and products. This office revolution not only has changed how work is done and information is handled but has redefined the function of everyone who works in an office, from the corporate executive down to the lowliest clerk...

7   For the job hunter of 2020, scanning[6] classified ads will be a quick education in how drastically[7] the workplace will have changed. He or she is likely to see openings for such positions as biological historians, biofarming experts, computer art curators, fiberoptics technicians, robot retrainers, space traffic controllers, and teleconferencing coordinators, to cite but a few.

8   There will always be farms, but by the next century farmworkers as we know them will be scarcer. The business of farming will become ever more complex. With computerized operations and robot harvesters, there will be no need for unskilled labor. The farm will be a place for people with training as electronic technicians, bioengineers, and computer programmers. Indeed, the human farmworker someday may be simply the person with the phone number of the nearest rebot repairman.

[5]**swollen:** enlarge; having got bigger
[6]**scanning:** looking over or reading quickly (often to find specific information)
[7]**drastically:** severely; suddenly

After You Read

● Identifying the Main Idea

DIRECTIONS: Choose the answer that best expresses the main idea.

1. Based on paragraphs 1 and 2, choose the statement that best expresses the main idea of the article.
    a. Industrialized nations will face many problems in the years ahead.
    b. New technological developments will greatly change our lives and the lives of our children.
    c. Robots will replace humans on factory production lines.
    d. Change is everywhere.

2. The main idea for the section "Job Markets and Careers" is:
    a. Our future world will be very different from today's world.
    b. Farmwork will be largely automated and computerized in the future.
    c. There will be more office jobs and fewer factory jobs in the future.
    d. New technology will create many new jobs and professions and will make many old ones outdated.

● Guessing Vocabulary from Context

When you encounter unfamiliar vocabulary in an English reading selection, what is your typical response? Do you bring out your bilingual or English monolingual dictionary to look up the word? Do you then spend precious moments looking through all the definitions to decide which one fits? Have you ever finally decided on a definition only to realize that you have forgotten what you were reading and must begin the sentence or paragraph all over again?

Over-reliance on a dictionary not only slows down your reading but may interfere with your comprehension as well. A better strategy is to use the **context**, the words and sentences surrounding a particular word, to help you **guess** that word's meaning. Usually the guesses you make will be accurate enough for you to understand the author's ideas. When they are not, or when the terms require an exact technical definition, you can use your English dictionary as a back-up resource.

DIRECTIONS: The following exercise contains words taken from the reading selection. Use the new context to select the most appropriate meaning.

1. Just as the invention of the automobile <u>rendered</u> horse-drawn carriages <u>obsolete</u> in modern cities, so the use of computers and word processors will make the common typewriter much <u>scarcer</u> in offices of the future.

    render obsolete: a.   cause it to be outdated and no longer useful
                           b.   cause it to increase in price
                           c.   cause it to change

scarcer: a. more common

                  b. more efficient

                  c. more rare

2. Because business computers are becoming more and more complex, many office workers have had to get new training to handle these <u>sophisticated</u> electronic systems.

sophisticated: a. complex

                b. business

                c. worldly

3. Computers are even becoming more <u>prevalent</u> in American schools and homes; perhaps in another twenty years every school-age child in the United States will be able to operate a computer.

prevalent: a. large

            b. common

            c. expensive

4. Some automobile factories have begun to <u>automate</u> their assembly lines by using robots instead of human workers. This <u>automation</u> will increase the amount of money needed for machinery but will decrease the cost of labor.

automate: a. to increase the number of human workers

            b. to produce a greater variety of products

            c. to operate or control something by machine rather than by human labor

automation: the noun form of *automate*, referring to the process of automating

5. Unlike white-collar workers, who usually work in an office, <u>blue-collar workers</u> may be found in many different work settings. For example, they may work outdoors to construct a new highway, or they may assemble new cars in an auto factory or repair damaged ones in a mechanic shop.

blue-collar workers: a. business executives

                      b. secretaries

                      c. manual laborers

6. The early industrial revolution contributed to the <u>demise</u> of the feudal lords and the rise of the bourgeoisie. Likewise, the new technological revolution may <u>herald</u> major social and economic changes in the societies of the future.

demise: a. creation

         b. loss of power

         c. gain in power

herald: a. introduce

         b. end

         c. respond to

7. Blue-collar workers were originally given this name because of the blue workshirts they often wore. Given this information and the preceding vocabulary clues, reread

paragraph 4. Can you guess what or who the "steel-collar workers" are who are replacing the blue-collar workers? Write your answer in the space provided.

steel-collar workers: _____

The Second Reading

Before You Read: Knowing Your Purpose

In the first reading you were looking for the main ideas of the article; this time, your purpose is to see how these ideas are supported. You might want to think about the following questions as you read:

1. What is the main change that will take place in the work force?
2. What types of jobs will be affected by this change?
3. What are some specific examples of the jobs and careers we might expect to see in the future?

After You Read

● Understanding the Author's Plan

In order to better understand what you read, it is often helpful to consider the author's plan of organization and method of development. In the following exercise, the purpose of each paragraph in the section "Job Markets and Careers" is explained in the left-hand column.

DIRECTIONS: Read each explanation and then answer the comprehension questions to the right.

Authors' Plan

Paragraph 3: states the main idea for this section: The new technological revolution will create many new jobs and make old jobs obsolete.

Paragraph 4: expands the main idea by defining the principal trend in the job market.

Paragraphs 4–8: discuss specific types of work and the expected developments in each.

Comprehension Questions

1. What kind of knowledge will the new jobs require workers to have?
2. What will happen to many of the existing jobs and skills?
3. Do the authors give examples of outdated jobs? What are they?
4. What is the most important change taking place in the American job market?
5. What will cause the "demise of the blue-collar worker?"
    Why?

Paragraph 4: examines factory work.

6. What has been the result of the automation which has already occurred in General Motors and U.S. Steel factories?

Paragraphs 5–6: discuss office work.

7. Will office and service jobs be plentiful or scarce in the future?
8. What kind of workers will be needed to fill these positions?
9. What is meant by the "paperless office?"
10. What two major developments have contributed to the growth of the paperless office?

Paragraph 7: introduces other new occupations of the future.

11. How do the examples given in paragraph 7 show the "drastic" change in the workplace? Choose one example and explain.

Paragraph 8: discusses farmwork.

12. Why will farmworkers as we know them be scarcer in the next century?
13. Who will perform the unskilled labor on the farms?

We can see that the authors have established a specific purpose for each paragraph. Recognizing the function of each paragraph helps us to understand the ideas presented in a reading.

● A Deeper Look: Discussion Questions

DIRECTIONS: Discuss the following questions in small groups. Compare your answers with those of your classmates.

1. The authors of "Our Future Stock" predict a greater demand for technically skilled labor and a decreased demand for unskilled labor. How do you think this will affect employment in industrialized nations? Have these effects already been seen in some areas?

2. How can the problem of displaced workers be resolved? Give examples.

3. In paragraph 2, the authors say, "the Third World countries will spearhead a new industrial age..." In a later section (not included in this textbook) they discuss several factors that will contribute to this advance in Third World countries. These factors include:
    —large populations
    —large amounts of unused resources
    —(in some cases) conservative governments that are opposed to labor legislation and antipollution laws.

Do you agree that these factors may contribute to rapid economic development in many developing countries? Why or why not? If possible, give examples of specific countries to support your view.

4. Have the technological advances mentioned in this article affected your nation or area? In what ways? What will these changes mean for your future?

5. Some critics of the new technology argue that if humans rely on computers and robots, we will become mentally lazy; we will lose our artistic creativity and our ability or desire to invent new ways of doing things. Do you agree? Why or why not?

● Becoming An Efficient Reader: Scanning

To scan is to read quickly to locate specific information or details.

On the next page is an imaginary Help Wanted section of the classified ads for the year 2020. The jobs listed in this section are based on the predictions made in the previous article and on other sources. The form of this ad section is similar to that used in many U.S. newspapers.

DIRECTIONS: Answer the following questions by scanning the Help Wanted ads. First, observe how the information is organized in the ads. Then, read each question carefully to understand what is being asked. To locate the information you need, move your eyes quickly over the printed page, paying particular attention to bold headlines and key words. Finally, write the answers in the spaces provided.

1. What is the date of this ad section?

2. Where is there a position open for a space traffic controller? How many jobs are available?

3. In order to be hired as the robot psychologist at West Docks Engineering Corporation, what experience must you have? Is this same experience required for the position at Robopsyche Institute?

4. If you enjoy working on a team with other robot psychologists, which position would you apply for?

5. If you are looking for training in a space-related field, which position would you apply for?

6. What benefits are available for new salespeople at Compu-Sales, Inc.? Is on-the-job training offered for this position?

7. What job is listed as a temporary position? How long will the job last? Is there a possibility that there will be a permanent job with this company in the future?

8. If you are a teleconferencing coordinator (TC) and you speak several languages, where might you apply for a job? What languages are required?

9. Which TC position requires experience with TeleTech Systems?

10. What position is available at Hayward State University? What qualifications are needed?

HELP WANTED: JOB OPPORTUNITIES

ROBOT PSYCHOLOGIST needed for scientific crew at West Docks Engineering Corp.
Responsibilities: to provide counseling and reprogramming to research robots suffering from directive overload and primary order conflict.
Qualifications: Must be independent and self-sufficient; able to get along without human companionship. B.S. in robotic psychology and experience with En500 Series robots required.
Process resumé to CompuStation 6Z, Entry #435592.

Are you a
ROBOT PSYCHOLOGIST
looking for a CHANGE?
Are you tired of working in isolation for a single company? Join the qualified professional team at

ROBOPSYCHE INSTITUTE.
a recently established research facility located in sunny San Jose, California. Enjoy working with stimulating colleagues while you receive excellent salary and career advancement opportunities.
All you need is a Master's degree in robotic psychology and a cooperative, energetic personality. We will provide additional training and on-the-job experience.
Process your resumé today to Robopsyche Institute, CompuStation 5C, Entry #41156.

TEMPORARY ROBOT RETRAINERS
NEEDED *NOW!*
600 Series-2Z3 Domestic Robots must be reprogrammed for new duties in a major San Francisco Hotel.
4-week deadline!
Programming degree and experience required. Good salary now with chance for permanent position to follow.
Call immediately: Elizabeth Cortex, personnel manager, 415-999-6443.

SALES/MARKETING: San Francisco-based firm is expanding business-computer operations. Needs 4 creative and energetic salespeople.
Qualifications: At least 2 years experience in computer sales; knowledge of "Value Star" and related business software.
Duties: Responsible for initiating new sales contacts and handling existing valued clients.
Benefits: Base salary + commission, health and dental insurance.
Apply now: Send resumé and current earnings statement to
COMPU-SALES, Inc.
CompuStation 9, Entry #6725

SPACE TRAFFIC CONTROLLER: 6 positions available for experienced space traffic controllers at the new space port in Santa Clara Valley. Excellent salary and benefits. Process resumé to CompuStation 9, Entry #4413.

SALES MANAGER: GFC, Inc. Agriculture Division. Knowledge of robot harvesters and agricultural operations software required. B.S. in Agricultural Management preferred. Send resumé and salary history to GFC, Inc., CompuStation 15, Entry #2195.

LOOKING FOR ADVENTURE?
Become a Space Geographer! On Oct. 9, Astro Travel, Inc. will begin a 4-month training session for space geographers: 3 months on-the-ground training in a classroom and 1 month actual space travel. Tuition includes travel expenses. Job placement guaranteed. Call 773-1212 for more information.

TELECONFERENCING COORDINATOR is being sought by major L.A.-based law firm. Must have experience with TeleTech systems, and T.C. training certificate. Call (213) 592-6312 for details.

TELECONFERENCING COORDINATOR: Trans-Po Bank and Trust Co. Energetic, efficient T.C. needed for international business conferences. Fluency in Spanish, Japanese, and English is a must. Experience with Tele-Tech systems preferred. Salary and benefits negotiable. Call (415) 599-6432.

UNIVERSITY PROFESSOR OF HISTORY FIELD: Early space exploration. Ph.D. in History with a concentration in international space programs. Send resumé and related publications to History Dept., Hayward State University, CompuStation 7, Entry #7924-0116.

16

Becoming a Proficient Writer

● Guided Writing: Considering Audience and Purpose

You have just scanned the classified ads and answered questions about them. Here is an exercise that will ask you to write about one of the ads.

DIRECTIONS: Look at the advertisement for a sales/marketing position. Imagine that you are the personnel manager for the company, Compu-sales, Inc. You need to send a note or memo (a short, informal letter, a memorandum) to the owner of the company describing the job that you are advertising. As you write, carefully consider the person *to whom* you are writing this note and *the reason* you are writing it. This will determine the style you use and the information you include. Your boss wants the description of this position to be written in paragraph form. You will need to include details about the required qualifications, and the duties and benefits of the job.

You might begin the memo like this:

To: Mr. John Wong, President
FROM: (your name), Personnel Manager

Our software division is looking for four new salespeople. We have placed an ad in the *Herald* describing the applicants' qualifications and the duties and benefits of the job.

_____

_____

_____

_____

_____

_____

_____

_____

_____

_____

Now, imagine that you are an applicant for this job and you have just received a call from the personnel manager with the good news that you have been hired. Write a letter to a friend describing your new job. Notice that this time you are writing for a very different reason and to a very different person than you did in the first paragraph. This time you will not include the same kind of detailed information about the job. However, you should include more specific information about the company than in the previous paragraph. Remember, your friend has never heard of Compusales, Inc.

You might begin like this:

Dear _____,

Guess what! I just got hired for a new job.

_____

_____

_____

_____

_____

_____

_____

_____

You will notice that the two paragraphs that you just wrote are quite different. Think about the person to whom you were writing these paragraphs and about your reasons for writing them. In the first paragraph you were writing to your boss to describe a position that he knew something about already. In the second paragraph you were writing to a friend to describe a job that he knew nothing about. The differences in these two paragraphs are a result of having different **audiences** (intended readers) and different **purposes** for your writing. You can see that the considerations of audience and purpose are very important in the writing process. They affect to a great extent what you choose to include, what you can leave out, the tone and style of the piece, and other important aspects of writing that we will focus on later in this text. You need to think about these two aspects of writing before you actually begin composing, as you write, and when you revise what you have written. More than any other considerations, audience and purpose shape writing.

LESSON 3

COMPOSING ON YOUR OWN

Throughout unit 1 you have been exploring ideas about work as it relates to our changing world. To do this you have used several different sources: **reading, brainstorming, groupwork,** and **freewriting**. Now you can use some of your ideas to write an essay.

Choosing a Topic

DIRECTIONS: Choose one of these topics to write a short composition about. Assume that you are writing this to share with your classmates.

A. Describe your present job. If you are not working, consider being a student as your job, or describe a former job or one that you are very familiar with. Then, tell either how this job has changed over the past ten years or how you expect it to change over the next twenty years.

B. Based on the kinds of changes and developments predicted in this unit or envisioned in your class, invent a possible job of the future. Use your imagination! Then write a paragraph describing this job in detail.

Note: Notice the difference between the possible purposes of the two choices. The purpose of topic A might be to inform. That of topic B might be to entertain. You might have a different purpose in mind. Whatever purpose you choose, consider how it will affect the essay.

Generating Ideas

To get started you can brainstorm, freewrite, or work in small groups to come up with ideas for this composition. Perhaps you already have your own method that helps you to explore your ideas. Use whatever method or combination of methods that, so far, has worked for you.

Writing the First Draft

Now it's time to begin writing the essay. Be sure to use the ideas that you thought of in the idea-generating exercise. You could also use these techniques to get started writing.

When writing, always keep your purpose and your audience in mind. They will determine, to a great extent, what you choose to include in your essay and the tone in which you write it.

Revising

After you have written your essay, reconsider it. Ask yourself if you have kept in mind your audience and your purpose.

Writing the Second Draft

Make any changes you would like to make. Before giving your paper to your teacher, reread it carefully to check for any errors.

Keeping a Journal

One enjoyable and productive way to develop writing skills is **journal writing**. Journal entries are always directly related to *you*. They may be about experiences, thoughts, feelings, or dreams that you have had. Since most of us find that it is easier to write about something that is familiar, we discover, in keeping a journal, a writing task that is comfortable.

Another aspect of journal writing that makes it an excellent device is its informal nature. Because keeping a journal gives you an opportunity to write *for yourself* and about yourself, you can choose an informal tone. (Remember our discussion of audience and purpose in this lesson.) An informal tone can help you to approach this writing task in a relaxed way. When you feel relaxed and comfortable, writing will seem more pleasant and easier. These positive feelings will encourage you to write more freely, which will help you to progress more quickly.

You will also discover that journal writing helps your writing in another way, by giving you more opportunities to write. The more frequently you write, the faster you will progress.

DIRECTIONS: Choose one of the following topics. Before you begin to write, give yourself some time to think about the ideas you have on this topic. You might use some of the techniques we have worked on in this unit to free the ideas you have about the topic. When you actually begin writing, try to relax. Remember that this is *your* journal. It is for *you*.

1. The year is 2020 A.D. You are writing in your personal diary. Today you have chosen to describe your job.
2. Discuss what you could resolve to do in the next year of your life that would help you to be better prepared for the future.
3. Write a letter to a friend telling him or her about why you are content or discontent with your present work or school situation.

UNIT TWO

AN EXPLODING POPULATION: DEMOGRAPHY

LESSON 1

THE POPULATION BOMB

About the Selection:

Our changing world is an important focus of attention in all scientific fields. The field of demography, the statistical study of human population, is no exception. Demographers are especially concerned with the effect that population changes will have on humanity. They have called attention to the rapid expansion of the world's population and have predicted that this population growth will create serious problems if it is not decreased. One well-known scientist, Dr. Paul R. Ehrlich, whose specialty is population biology, finds these predictions particularly alarming. In the following excerpt from his famous book, *The Population Bomb*, he describes a personal experience he had that made him acutely aware of the dangers of over-population.

As You Read: Looking for the General Ideas

As you read this descriptive excerpt, try to envision what Dr. Ehrlich meant by his closing reference to "the feeling of overpopulation." Remember to use the reading techniques you learned in unit 1. Several quick, purposeful readings, in which you don't worry about vocabulary, will be more effective than one slow reading for details.

THE POPULATION BOMB
by Dr. Paul Ehrlich

I have understood the population explosion intellectually for a long time. I came to understand it emotionally one stinking hot night in Delhi a couple of years ago. My wife and daughter and I were returning to our hotel in an ancient taxi. The seats were hopping with fleas. The only functional gear was third. As we crawled through the city, we entered a crowded slum area. The temperature was well over 100, and the air was a haze of dust and smoke. The streets seemed alive with people. People eating, people washing, people sleeping. People visiting, arguing, and screaming. People thrusting their hands through the taxi window, begging. People defecating and urinating. People clinging to buses. People herding animals. People, people, people, people. As we moved slowly through the mob, hand horn squawking, the dust, noise, heat, and cooking fires gave the scene a hellish aspect. Would we ever get to our hotel? All three of us were, frankly, frightened. It seemed that anything could happen—but, of course, nothing did. Old India hands will laugh at our reaction. We were just some overprivileged tourists, unaccustomed to the sights and sounds of India. Perhaps, but since that night I've known the *feel* of overpopulation.

From *The Population Bomb, Revised Edition*, by Paul R. Ehrlich, Jr. Copyright © 1968, 1971 by Paul R. Ehrlich. Reprinted by permission of Ballantine Books, a Division of Random House Inc.

After You Read

• Discovering the Main Idea

DIRECTIONS: Answer the following questions, which will help you to better understand the main idea of the reading.

1. Where does this story occur? Be as specific as possible.
2. Who is the storyteller with?
3. Where were the author and his companions going? How were they getting there?
4. What section of the city did the taxi have to pass through to get to the hotel?
5. What scene did the author observe from the taxi?
6. How did the scene make the author and his family feel?

7. Did anything bad actually happen to the author and his family?
8. What did that night help the author to understand?

Notice that your answer to question 8 tells you, in a general way, what the article is about. You have discovered the **main idea** of this article.

● Seeing Through the Author's Eyes

This real-life moment described by Dr. Ehrlich gives the reader a vivid picture of his experience. The following questions should help you to understand how he shares his experience with you, how he draws you into the atmosphere of his unforgettable night in Delhi.

DIRECTIONS: Refer to the article by Dr. Ehrlich to find answers to the following questions. You might choose to work with a classmate for this exercise.

1. The author tells you that the night in Delhi was "stinking hot." What other evidence does he give you later to show you that this is true?
2. He tells you that the taxi is old. What details does he add immediately that help you to picture the "ancient taxi"?
3. The author labels the area he passes through as "a crowded slum area."
   a. He repeats the word *people* many times. What impression does the repetition of this word leave on you?
   b. What verbs does he use to describe the people's actions that lead you to agree that the area was a slum (a filthy district inhabited by the poor)?
4. He is worried that something bad could happen, and he tells us that he and his family are frightened. What question does he ask that shows us that he is feeling concerned about their safety?

Dr. Ehrlich has given us an opportunity to share his experience by describing an overcrowded scene without explicitly stating that there were many people. Yet we can *feel* what he felt, the oppressive crush of hundreds of people. He has led us into drawing conclusions about the scene. Our conclusions are the same as his, that overpopulation can create devastating effects. When a writer gives us enough facts and evidence to form the impressions he wants us to form, to "see" the picture he wants us to see, we say that the writer is **showing**, not telling.

● Understanding Showing: Working in Pairs

Now you will have an opportunity to use your answers to the preceding questions to see *how* Dr. Ehrlich uses showing.

DIRECTIONS: Use your answers to the preceding exercise to complete the column marked "Showing" in the following chart. The first details are filled in for you.

Telling (label/conclusion)	Showing (evidence/details/facts)
stinking hot night in Delhi	—100 degrees —haze of dust and smoke
ancient taxi	— — —
crowded slum	— — — — — — —

Now, use only the information in the "Telling" column to complete the following statement:

The author drove through___ _____

_____   _____

_____   _____

_____   _____ .

Is this statement as convincing to you as the paragraph written by Dr. Ehrlich? Of course not. These simple judgments do not necessarily convince us of their truth. We are more convinced by facts that lead us to make conclusions on our own. When we add the information under "Showing," we believe these judgments because we have had an opportunity to judge the facts on our own. Dr. Ehrlich does not just tell us. He shows.

Becoming a Proficient Writer

Generating Ideas

● Freewriting

You have just carefully examined a piece of writing in which the writer painted a picture of a scene that left a strong impression on him. Now you will have an opportunity to write about a scene that left a strong impression on *you*. Later, you will share what you have written with a classmate.

DIRECTIONS: Close your eyes. Look back in time. Search your memory for a scene in your past experiences that left a strong impression on you. You might have witnessed a scene yesterday that sticks out in your mind. Perhaps you will remember scenes from your past or your childhood. Let these images flash through your mind, one after another. Now, try to settle your mind on one. Write a name for that scene at the top of a sheet of paper. Try to visualize it as you think about what overall impression the scene left you with. Think about what you saw, smelled, heard, and felt that left you with this impression. Now, begin writing. Remember to use the freewriting techniques we talked about in unit 1. Write for ten minutes without stopping. Don't lift your pen from your paper. Don't judge your ideas or worry about the technical aspects of your writing. Have fun writing!

● Looping

You have had an opportunity to freewrite about a scene you once observed. Now you will use that freewriting to generate further ideas on this topic.

DIRECTIONS: Using your freewriting, follow these steps.

1. Reread what you wrote, underlining any sentences or phrases in your freewriting that appeal to you and interest you.
2. Decide which one of these underlined ideas appeals to you the most. Try to choose an idea that you have something further to write about.
3. Write this new topic at the top of a sheet of paper.
4. Again, freewrite, focusing on the specific topic that you have chosen. Remember to follow the procedure for freewriting. If you think you have run out of things to write, don't stop! Write about what you are thinking as you try to get back to your topic.
5. When you are finished, freewrite on either another area that you underlined in your first freewriting, or on a new area of interest that emerged from your second (focused) freewriting. Keep in mind your freewriting techniques! Your pen should move continuously for seven to ten minutes. Does this sound difficult? The more you do it, the easier it gets. Relax and enjoy it!

This process, called **looping**, is another way to free your thoughts. It is designed to help you to find "hot spots" in your writing, areas that generate further ideas. These areas might spark a flame that will kindle a fire burning bright with ideas that you never knew you had!

● Expanding Ideas to Show

Now let's examine your freewritings in terms of what you have learned about showing. When you reread your freewriting, can you locate examples of telling in which you simply made a judgment about what you saw? Can you locate examples of showing, places where you gave details, facts, evidence to help the reader to form the same impression you had of the scene? The following activity will help you to determine where your writing uses telling and showing.

DIRECTIONS: For this activity you will read the writing of one classmate to look for examples of showing and telling. Before beginning, review the sections in this lesson on showing, and then, choose one of the three pieces of writing you have just completed to share with your classmate.

1. Begin by reading your partner's freewriting while he or she reads yours.
2. Together, go over one of the freewritings, sentence by sentence, to find where the writer used labels, judgments, or conclusions. Underline these examples of telling. Number each example.
3. Consider the first example of telling, labeled with a number 1. Go back over the writing to find examples of showing, details, facts, evidence, that support this first example of telling. Circle these examples and label them with a number 1.
4. For each numbered example of telling, locate and number corresponding examples of showing.
5. Find examples of telling that have no showing to support them. Point these out to the writer.
6. Repeat this process for the other student's paper.

If you have located places in your writing where you used telling only, choose one example which would be enhanced by adding showing detail. Write the full sentence containing this example on a sheet of paper. Now, try adding showing details. You might do this by adding words, phrases, or clauses to the same sentence or by adding new sentences to the original. When you have finished, show this to your partner.

LESSON 2

THE WORLD'S URBAN EXPLOSION

About the Selection:

In lesson 1 you read about how one man experienced the "feel" of overpopulation. Dr. Ehrlich's experience was a powerful moment for him; it intensified his concern for the problems that overpopulation could create for the entire world, a concern shared by many. To help you to further explore this issue, we present the next reading, "The World's Urban Explosion," by Robert J. Fox. This article from the *National Geographic* magazine presents facts, figures, and predictions that shed light on this problem.

The First Reading

As You Read: Looking for the Main Idea

To understand the main idea, look for answers to the following questions:

1. What is the projected world population for the year 2025?
2. Where will the greatest population increases occur?
3. What current problems in some overcrowded urban areas might the population explosion make worse?

THE WORLD'S URBAN EXPLOSION
by Robert W. Fox

1   By the reckoning of my fellow demographers[1], human population first reached one billion in the early 19th century. But it took little more than another hundred years for that figure to climb to two billion in 1930, and by 1975 the number doubled again. In the remaining years of this century world population will top six billion; by 2025, eight billion.

2   The lion's share of this increase will occur in the emerging nations, already home to most of mankind, and will be concentrated in cities overburdened by their current populations. Advances in technology and medicine that allow us longer, healthier lives have buoyed[2] population size and growth rate—and thus created challenges of magnitudes the world has never before faced.

3   Urban authorities worldwide are declaring their regions to be in crisis situations with drastic[3] shortcomings in housing, water, sewage, transportation, and job opportunities. Lagos, Nigeria, for example, with some five million people and one of the world's highest growth rates, has so far been unsuccessful in planning construction of a citywide sewer system.

4   Urban areas in developing countries are haphazardly spreading far beyond traditional boundaries to accommodate natural population increase and rural migration. Industrial and residential uses and speculation often take over valuable farmland. On the edges of Cairo, prime agricultural land is being lost to the destructive stripping of topsoil for brickmaking.

5   Rapid population growth and urbanization will continue into the foreseeable future, with bleak[4] consequences. Conditions today are only the opening scenes of a drama in which Third World cities, now home to more than one billion people, will hold nearly four billion residents by 2025.

The Urbanization Trend In Developing Nations

6   Only seven urban centers held more than five million in 1950: New York, London, Paris, Germany's Rhein-Ruhr com-

[1]**demographers:** scientists studying human population.
[2]**buoyed:** maintained.
[3]**drastic:** severe.
[4]**bleak:** gloomy.

plex, Tokyo-Yokohama, Shanghai, and Buenos Aires. Labor supply and demand had grown in unison[5] as these centers evolved over decades, if not centuries. The enduring[6] architecture of London and Paris reflects slow, graceful development.

7   Today 34 cities boast more than five million residents. By 2025, the UN projects, there will be 93, and 80 of these will be in the emerging nations. Leisurely development and a low to moderate population growth rate are luxuries of the past.

8   The upsurge in Third World urban populations has overwhelmed resources. Sprawling slums, massive traffic jams, chronic unemployment, regular failure of electric and water services, strained educational and recreational facilities, and skyrocketing food and fuel costs are the stuff of daily existence.

9   Though demographers warned that the population of Mexico City would double during the 1970s, few others believed such a rise could occur. Yet the metropolis did grow from 8 million to 14 million people, and it may reach 30 million by 2000. Similar projections for other developing nations are now being accepted as realistic.

The Paradox Of Population Growth

10   For most of mankind's history world population grew slowly, checked by epidemics, famine, and chronic malnutrition. Though the mortality[7] rate was high, the birthrate was slightly higher, and with that small excess our numbers gradually increased.

11   Human population grows much like a savings account accruing[8] compound interest—greater amounts yield greater amounts. English economist Thomas Malthus cited this fact in his 1798 "Essay on the Principal of Population," warning that human numbers—if unchecked—would soon outweigh the ability of the earth to feed them.

12   But Malthus was writing on the eve of a new era, when the industrial revolution would transform Europe. The continent's population did rise substantially during the 19th century as medical breakthroughs lowered the death rate, but simultaneous agricultural advances also allowed food production to rise. And emigration to America helped siphon off[9] population excess.

13   The newly widened gap between birth and death rates gradually began to close as smaller families become socially acceptable. That trend quickened in industrialized countries during the 20th century, and today the gap between births and deaths is once again small.

14   In the developing countries a far different history prevails. Only in the 1930s did the death rate begin to fall, but it fell dramatically as imported technology improved overall health and dietary conditions. The birthrate, however, remained high. Its decline depends largely on changing cultural norms, and family planning has made substantial inroads only within the past two decades. As the gap between deaths and births widened, the population exploded. Generally speaking, there were not more births—there were more survivors.

15   With this considerable momentum,[10] population expansion in these countries

[5]**in unison:** simultaneously.
[6]**enduring:** lasting.
[7]**mortality:** death.
[8]**accruing:** increasing.
[9]**siphon off:** draw off or diminish.
[10]**momentum:** impetus.

will continue. Even optimistic scenarios do not foresee a leveling off of growth until late in the 21st century.

[16] Because the traditional birth-and-death-rate relationship has been broken in Third World countries only within the past few decades, they now hold very youthful populations, and the populations will continue to soar because there are more women of childbearing age. Hence the paradox of modern population growth: Even as the birthrate continues to fall, the population will rise.

[17] For every 100 Africans today, 55 are under 20 years of age. Among Europeans only 30 out of 100 are under 20. In 1975, 93 million African women were of childbearing age. The birthrate that year in Africa was 47 per 1,000, and 19 million children were born. The UN projects that by 2025 the African birthrate will fall to 25 per 1,000—a reduction of almost half. But by then the number of reproductive-age women will have risen to 430 million, and even with a lowered birthrate 42 million children will enter the world that year.

A Clouded Crystal Ball

[18] How many people can the earth hold? Will birth and death rates continue to decline? Can food production keep apace of population growth? Can technology supplement or replace today's resources? What are the long-term effects of pollution on health, climate, and farm production?

[19] Debate over such issues has spawned volumes, as scholars look to the future with varying degrees of optimism and gloom. In a lecture titled "The Terror of Change," Patricia Gulas Strauch cited three aspects of our future about which there is little disagreement: The speed of change will accelerate, the world will be increasingly complex, and nations and world issues will be increasingly interdependent.

[20] The problems facing Third World megacities cannot be ignored by developed countries. We cannot look to the past for solutions; there is no precedent for such growth. We are in uncharted, challenging waters.

Excerpts from "The World's Urban Explosion" by Robert W. Fox. First published in *National Geographic*, August 1984. Copyright © 1984 Robert W. Fox. Reprinted by permission of the author.

After You Read

• Discovering the Main Idea

The following questions will help you to further understand the major issues raised in the reading.

DIRECTIONS: Choose the appropriate answer.

1. Advances in technology and medicine have helped increase the population growth because
    a. we are now richer.
    b. we live in a more challenging world.
    c. we can live longer.

2. Cities can expect to
    a. continue developing gracefully.
    b. suffer because of rapid population growth.
    c. halt population increases.

3. The gap between birth rates and death rates has increased
    a. in industrialized nations.
    b. worldwide.
    c. in developing countries.
4. According to the author, the problems created by overpopulation
    a. should be everyone's concern.
    b. concern Third World countries principally.
    c. are impossible to solve.

● Guessing Vocabulary from Context

In unit 1 we encouraged you to rely on contextual meaning for unfamiliar vocabulary. Did you resist the temptation to pull out your bilingual dictionary to answer the vocabulary questions in unit 1? Have you referred to your dictionary in the reading in this lesson? Learning how to guess a new word's meaning from its context can take some practice. Here's another chance to sharpen your skill at this.

DIRECTIONS: Guess the meaning of the word in parentheses, using the same kinds of clues that you used in unit 1. You might figure out the meaning by referring to the words and sentences around the vocabulary word or by using grammatical clues such as articles or word endings. Then find a word or words in the list of possibilities that has a similar meaning. Write the answer in the space provided.

1. The lion's share of this increase will occur in the _____ nations,
    (emerging)
    already home to most of mankind, and will be concentrated in cities _____
    (overburdened)
    by their current populations.

2. _____ in developing countries are _____ spreading far
    (urban areas)   (haphazardly)
    beyond traditional boundaries to _____ natural population increases
    (accommodate)
    and rural _____.
    (migration)

    provide for   cities
    population resettling   developing
    without a plan or pattern   strained

3. _____ development and a low to moderate population growth rate
    (leisurely)
    are _____ of the past.
    (luxuries)

4. _____ slums, _____ traffic jams, _____
    (sprawling)   (massive)   (chronic)

unemployment, regular failure of electric and water services, strained educational

and recreational facilities, and _____ food and fuel costs are the stuff
                                        (skyrocketing)

of daily existence.

very large	spread out
slow	rapidly rising
continuing for a long time	comforts

The Second Reading

As You Read: Understanding How the Parts Make Up a Whole

To understand how the writer gets his message across to the reader, we can look at how he proves his main point. To do this we must first see how he assigns a different purpose to each section of the reading. Because of the special nature of the first and last sections of this four-part reading, we have filled in their purposes. Can you figure out the main idea of the two middle sections? After rereading the article write the main idea in the blanks.

1. Section 1 serves as an introduction, presenting the projections of the population explosion in Third World urban centers and the problems resulting from such a situation.

2. Section 2 _____

3. Section 3 _____

4. Section 4 serves as a conclusion, restating the problem, presenting further questions that we might ask ourselves, and encouraging all readers to consider this as a problem that they should be concerned about.

You have just analyzed how each section serves a special purpose and helps to prove the main idea. Now we can examine one of these sections to see how the author further convinces us that his main idea is valid.

After You Read

● Showing with Facts and Statistics

The article you have just read raises issues of great concern for humankind. We, as readers, are left with a sense of responsibility. What makes us respond this way? How does the writer convince us that the situation is as alarming as he claims? What makes his predictions so believable?

In lesson 1, we learned that one key to writing powerful description is *showing*. We can apply this same basic idea to articles like the one you read in lesson 2. Let's examine how the writer has applied this concept to make his writing convincing.

Look back at section 2 of the reading, "The Urbanization Trend in Developing Nations." We can see how the information in this section must be convincing in order to make the rest of the article believable. If we don't believe that there will be a population explosion in urban centers, the writer might just as well not have written this article! The last paragraph (¶9) is the key to making the reader accept that this is probably going to happen.

DIRECTIONS: Reread paragraph 9, and answer the following questions.

1. What prediction did demographers make about population growth in Mexico City in the 1970s?
2. Did most people believe this would happen?
3. What actually *did* happen?
4. What prediction does the author mention about the population growth of Mexico City for the year 2000?
5. Does the author claim that most people now accept similar predictions for other emerging countries?
6. Do you believe these predictions? Why or why not?

The author has convinced us by showing us that predictions for the past came true even though many people didn't expect them to. He proved this by giving us actual **facts** and **statistics**. It is a fact, a truth, that demographers, who are experts, made such predictions. It is a fact that many people didn't believe these predictions. The statistics (facts presented as numbers) in this article show us that the predictions were not far from what really happened. The earlier predictions came true, so we expect the expert's new predictions also to come true. The writer has done his job well.

Keep in mind that the intended audience and purpose play an essential role in the author's decisions as to what kind of details he uses to prove his point. For whom do you think the article is written? What do you think the author's purpose is? How do you think this relates to his decision to use facts and statistics?

● Facts and Statistics: Understanding Graphic Illustrations

As we discovered in the preceding exercise, the writer convinced the readers by including facts and statistics in the body paragraphs. Another way to introduce this type of support is by using **graphic illustrations** or, simply, **graphics** in the form of diagrams, tables, maps, flowcharts, or graphs. By looking at one graphic we can understand the complex interrelationships between many facts and figures.

DIRECTIONS: To understand how the following graphic helps to convince you that the main point is true, answer the following questions by referring to the information in the graph. Use the prereading techniques you have learned; begin by reading the title, the introductory material in italics, the footnotes, and the labels of the columns.

Twin booms in overall and urban population show their impact in these bar graphs illustrating growth patterns in industrialized countries on the left and in developing nations on the right.

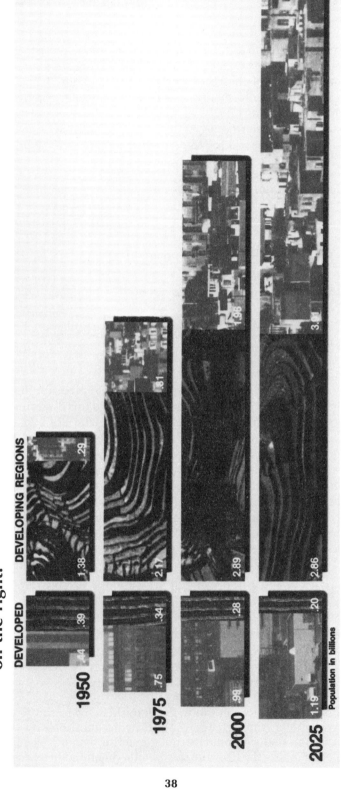

DEVELOPED

DEVELOPING REGIONS

1950   .44   .39   1.38   .29

1975   .75   .34   2.1   .81

2000   .99   .28   2.89   1.96

2025   1.19   .20   2.86   3.01

Population in billions

Graphics by Allen Carroll. © National Geographic Society.

38

1. What is the graph about?
2. What kind of countries are represented by the bars on the left side of the graph? On the right?
3. What years does the graphic present information about?
4. Each bar has two sections. What does each section represent? How do you know?
5. What do the numbers at the bottom of each bar represent?
6. What conclusion do you draw after examining this graph?

We can see that this graph paints a convincing picture of predictions about population growth in the urban areas of developing countries. Now, write one sentence that summarizes the information in this graphic. When you make a summary statement, use the details, the facts and statistics, to draw a conclusion, but eliminate them from the statement itself. Your statement should tell and not show.

The bar graph shows that _____

_____

_____

_____

● Supporting Detail: Analyzing Graphic Illustrations

Graphics can take many forms. Following is another type of graphic material, a map, which relates to the urban population article. You will work in a small group with a few classmates to analyze the information in this graphic.

DIRECTIONS: Analyze the graphic by answering the following questions. Your group should appoint a secretary to take notes and a reporter to share your findings with the rest of the class. Remember to use prereading techniques.

1. What does the title suggest that the graphic is about?
2. The map compares statistics in two different ways.
    a. What two years are being compared?
    b. What two types of countries are being compared?
3. Why do you think the map of the year 2025 is so much bigger than the map of the year 1984?
4. Why are some of the horizontal lines longer than others?
5. What conclusion do you draw from the information given in the graphic?

Your group's reporter should write the answer to question 5 on the board. The class should compare each group's conclusion and decide which ones are the best.

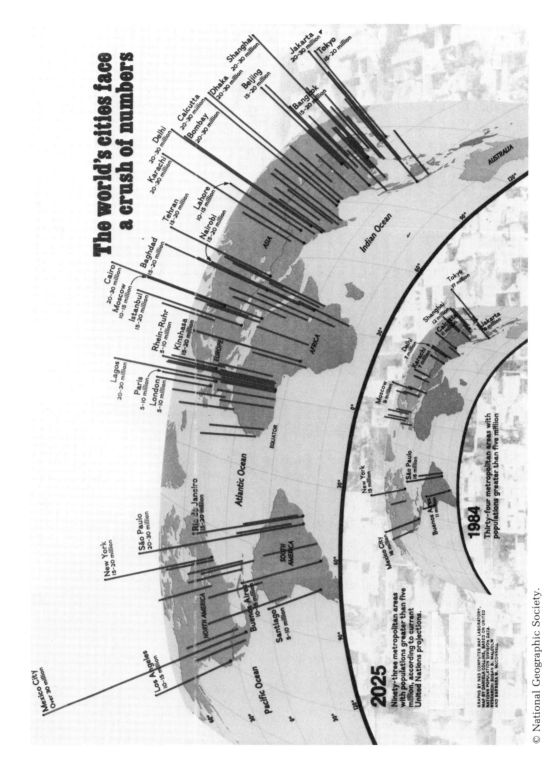

The world's cities face a crush of numbers

Mexico City
Over 30 million

Los Angeles
10-15 million

New York
15-20 million

São Paulo
20-30 million

Rio de Janeiro
15-20 million

Buenos Aires
10-15 million

Santiago
5-10 million

Lagos
20-30 million

Paris
5-10 million

London
5-10 million

Rhein-Ruhr
5-10 million

Kinshasa
15-20 million

Cairo
20-30 million

Moscow
10-15 million

Istanbul
15-20 million

Baghdad
15-20 million

Tehran
15-20 million

Nairobi
15-20 million

Lahore
10-15 million

Karachi
20-30 million

Delhi
20-30 million

Bombay
20-30 million

Calcutta
20-30 million

Dhaka
20-30 million

Shanghai
20-30 million

Beijing
15-20 million

Bangkok
15-20 million

Jakarta
20-30 million

Tokyo
15-20 million

Pacific Ocean

Atlantic Ocean

Indian Ocean

NORTH AMERICA

SOUTH AMERICA

EUROPE

AFRICA

ASIA

AUSTRALIA

EQUATOR

2025

Ninety-three metropolitan areas with populations greater than five million, according to current United Nations projections.

1984

Thirty-four metropolitan areas with populations greater than five million.

Mexico City
18 million

New York
15 million

São Paulo
16 million

Buenos Aires
11 million

Moscow
8 million

Delhi
7 million

Karachi
6 million

Shanghai
12 million

Calcutta
11 million

Jakarta
8 million

Tokyo
17 million

GRAPHS BY NGS COMPUTER MAP LABORATORY,
WITH JOHN AGNOTTA, BASED ON UNITED
NATIONS POPULATION DIVISION DATA.
RESEARCH BY MARGARET G. ZACKOWITZ
AND BARBARA MCCONNELL

40

Becoming a Proficient Writer

Guided Writing: Using Facts and Statistics from Graphics

Now that your class has agreed on a conclusion, let's go back in the other direction. You began examining the information presented in the graphic by looking at the details. From there you drew a conclusion which summarized the main point of the map. Now let's write a paragraph beginning with the main point and using the details in the graphic to prove the point and to develop the paragraph.

DIRECTIONS: Write a paragraph using the following steps.

1. Make the conclusion the first sentence of your paragraph.
2. Use details from the graphic to further explain the conclusion. You don't need to use all of the details, but your paragraph will be more interesting and certainly more convincing if you include some specific examples.
3. Consider each detail
   a. to make sure that you have only used details that are relevant, that help to prove the point.
   b. to see if you explained clearly how each detail helps to prove the point.

LESSON 3

COMPOSING
ON YOUR OWN

In this unit you have read about the issues surrounding the predicted population explosion. You have also worked with important writing techniques such as showing and using facts and statistics. Let's now try to apply what you have learned to the writing process.

The First Draft

Choosing a Topic

DIRECTIONS: Choose one of the following topics to write about in a paragraph.

A. Explain the information introduced in the following bar graph.

B. In the final paragraphs of the article "The World's Urban Explosion," the author raises the question of what the effects of the population explosion might be in the future. Imagine your city, town, or village in the year 2025. Imagine that the population predictions did, in fact, come true. Place yourself in the scene, and describe what you see.

Note: Notice how different these topics are from one another. The first topic asks you to write an explanation which analyzes a graph. The second topic asks for a

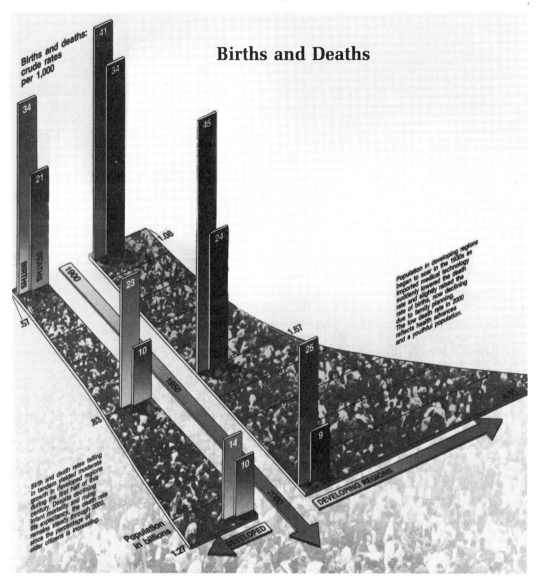

Births and Deaths

Graphics by Allen Carroll. © National Geographic Society.

description. Think about the possible purposes of each topic. How do you think these purposes will affect the tone of each piece?

Generating Ideas

First, we need to find ways to unlock the hidden ideas we have in our minds. In this unit you have learned to use brainstorming, freewriting, and looping. Try these techniques in any combination that works for you. Reading also helps to generate ideas. As you write, keep in mind the information you learned about this topic in the readings.

Writing the First Draft

After exploring your ideas, put them into paragraph form, keeping in mind how showing and using facts and statistics makes writing powerful and convincing. Our task here is to discover how we can best express our ideas in the clearest manner possible so that our readers will receive the same message, with the same impact, that we intended.

Peerediting

What follows is an element of the writing process that is especially important: sharing what we have written with others, our readers, to see if we have been successful in conveying our intended meaning. This step can be a fascinating adventure. We step out of our own selves, to see what we have created through the eyes of others, to discover the impact of our words on the thoughts of our readers, so that we can then use this information to *improve* what we have written. We call this **peerediting**.

Peerediting is a true sharing process. Not only do you get feedback from your classmates, but you also give feedback to them. It is a two-way street. You learn to be a better writer *and* a better reader. In the following exercise you will work with several classmates, taking the roles of both reader and writer.

DIRECTIONS: Work with a group of four other classmates who chose to write on the same topic as you did.

1. Discuss the idea-generating techniques that you each used to write this composition.
2. Read each other's papers silently, and answer the following questions for each paper:
    a. What do you like the most about the writing?
    b. What is the main idea?
    c. Who is the audience, and what is the purpose?
    d. What convincing details does the writer use?
    e. Where could the writer add details to make the piece more convincing?
    f. What areas in the writing seem unclear?
    g. How could the writer make the piece clearer?
3. Now, for each paper, compare your notes on the questions to help the writer think of ways to improve the piece.

Revising

You have gotten feedback about your composition from several classmates. Now you can use what you learned about your writing to improve it, to make it clearer and more convincing. Writers call this step of the process **revising**. All good writers go through several steps of revision because they want to make their writing the best it can be. At this point they reconsider what they have written, get feedback from others, and then make changes.

Review your notes from your peerediting session. Think about the comments made by your peerreaders; in particular, comments they agreed on. *If* you agree with them, you can revise the piece. Remember, however, that *you* are the final judge as to what you want to include or eliminate in your writing.

Make corrections directly on your first draft. Do not be afraid to mark up this paper. You can scratch out unnecessary or irrelevant information, squeeze ideas that you want to add into the margin, and even cut up and repaste your paper to change the order or make additions. You might be surprised to see the revising process of professional writers. Their drafts will often be illegible to anyone but themselves!

The Second Draft

Writing the Second Draft and Proofreading

Once you have made the necessary changes in your paper, you can rewrite it legibly. As you are rewriting, you may think of more changes that you would like to make. Do not hesitate to continue revising during this step. Writing takes time and a lot of thought, so take advantage of this stage to keep improving what you have already done. After you have rewritten your paper, go over it carefully to see if the language sounds correct and if your message seems complete and understandable. Finally, submit your paper to your teacher.

Using Your Teacher's Feedback

When your paper is returned to you, spend time examining the comments your teacher made. This is a good time to compare your classmates' responses to your teacher's, taking into account the changes you made between the original draft and the revised paper. Did you improve on the parts of your original paper that your classmates encouraged you to work on? Did your teacher comment on aspects of your paper that your classmates did not comment on? Share this information with the classmates you did peerediting with. For each paper you looked at, compare the comments you made to the teacher's comments. Keep in mind the ideas you and your teacher had in common about each paper. Also, notice comments that your teacher made that you missed. This is valuable information. You'll use it the next time you write and the next time you do peerediting.

Keeping a Journal

In this unit we read about population growth, about changes that we expect to take place in the future that will affect our lives. For a moment, reflect back in time. Try to visualize a place from your distant past, any place that sticks out in your mind. Now roll the clock back up to the present. If the place looks very different in the present, you've found your journal topic. If not, start again until you come up with a scene that has changed over a period of time. When you've found this place that has changed, write about it. You can choose to describe it as it was in the past, in the present, or you can do both. You might want to write about how the changes in the place have affected you. Whatever aspect of the place you choose to write about, make sure that you have a single purpose, a central focus, and try to include detail that helps to develop that main point only. Remember that when you choose to write about something that is familiar and important to you, the task of writing is easier and more pleasurable.

UNIT THREE

MAN AND THE COSMOS: ASTRONOMY

LESSON 1

BETWEEN FIRE AND ICE: THE PLANETS

About the Selection:

Since the beginning of our time on this planet, people's eyes have wandered toward the heavens, drinking in the vastness, asking the questions: Why? How? When? In the past, our search for answers came from the strong feelings that the unknown heavens awoke in us and from our own vast imagination. Thus, events in the skies became stories about gods: their loves, their struggles, their triumphs and defeats. Today, however, science is beginning to explain some of these events and mysteries. How, we might wonder, has this scientific progress affected our feelings about our universe?

In this excerpt from "Between Fire and Ice: The Planets," *National Geographic* writer Rick Gore touches on this question as he describes the first time he saw a total eclipse of the sun. Gore, a man of science, had the modern knowledge to explain this event. Yet, curiously enough, he experienced the same feelings our ancestors might have experienced on such an occasion.

Before You Read: Exploring Your Own Ideas

Can you remember the last time you looked up into the night sky? What did you see there? What were your feelings and thoughts as your eyes pierced the blackness above you? Take a minute to reflect on your experience. Now explore your thoughts briefly in freewriting.

BETWEEN FIRE AND ICE: THE PLANETS
by Rick Gore

1   On June 11, 1983, at 9:53 a.m. a distant siren could be heard in the village of Patuk on Java. Moments later, Asmo Wiyono began to strike the *kentongan*, the hand-carved, wooden chime-like alarm that hangs near his thatch home. Usually the kentongan warns villagers of thieves or erupting volcanoes. This day it signaled the onset of the *gerhana matahari*—Java's first total eclipse of the sun in a century.

2   This is my first total eclipse as well. I have come to Java for the poetry and symbolism this most basic of solar system phenomena promises. It will also inaugurate a mission.

3   For years, as a journalist, I have been reporting on our exploration of the planets. Over the past two decades we, the human race, have landed our machines on the moon, Mars, and Venus. We have

Eugene Gordon

braved the violent electromagnetic aura around Jupiter and photographed its puzzling moons. We have flown with awesome precision through the rings of Saturn and sent a spacecraft out toward the boundaries of our sun's domain. Our Pioneers and Vikings and Voyagers have probed and sampled and analyzed. Now I am struggling to synthesize what we have learned.

4   Yet that high-tech universe seems so far away this morning as I sip tea in Asmo Wiyono's home and watch a pinhole in his thatch roof cast a crescent image of the disappearing sun on his granddaughter's face.

5   "My grandmothers and my father have told me this story of eclipses," Wiyono says. "They are caused by Betara Kala, an ugly, giant son of god who was thrown out of heaven. He is trying to eat the sun in his vengeful anger. I know this is not modern thinking. But we think if we make enough noise, we can scare the giant away."

6   It takes an hour and a half for Betara Kala to eat the sun. As totality approaches, the women in Wiyono's family begin to sing. With broomlike pestles they noisily beat their canoe-size *lesung*, or rice mortar. Torches are lit and the clatter of kentongans resounds across the countryside.

7   An eerie dusk descends, and for five minutes the moon's disk creates a phantasmagoric[1] black hole in the sky. Radiant silver-white flares shoot out from the darkened sun. Venus and Mars both emerge in this untimely evening. A mild earthquake sets the ground atremble, and I am tempted briefly to believe in giants.

8   Totality ends and an abrupt sunrise erases the planets. The noisy ritual in the village ceases. Life wins. I return to the world of science. But for a moment the myths that still live on Java have accented just how far we have come, in much less than one generation, in comprehending the solar system.

[1]**phantasmagoric:** dream-like, rapidly changing.

From National Geographic, January 1985. © 1985 National Geographic Society.

After You Read

• Vocabulary From Context: Identifying Words With Precise Meanings

DIRECTIONS: Read the paragraph indicated to find the words with the following meanings.

A. Verbs

1. Find the word in paragraph 1 that means "violently bursting forth" or "ejecting matter." _____

2. Find the word in paragraph 2 that means "to begin; to initiate." _____

3. What word in paragraph 3 means "to combine separate abstract entities or ideas into a single or unified conclusion"? _____

4. What word in paragraph 6 means "to make an echoing sound" or "to sound loudly"? _____

B. Nouns

5. What word in paragraph 2 means "observable facts, occurrences, or circumstances"? _____

6. Find the word in paragraph 6 that means "an instrument used for pounding or grinding." _____

C. Adjectives

7. What word in paragraph 1 refers to something made of straw or leaves?

_____

8. In paragraph 5, find the synonym for "vindictive; desiring to inflict a wrong or injury on someone in return for one received." _____

9. In paragraph 7, what is the synonym for "shaking"? _____

10. Find the synonym in paragraph 8 for "sudden." _____

• Comprehending a Sequence: Verb Tense Clues

One reason that stories are so popular in all cultures is that they are generally easy to follow. The events of a story are usually told in the order in which they occur—usually, but not always. Sometimes an author may vary his or her style by presenting the incidents out of their natural order. Then we as readers must rely on other clues to understand the true sequence of events.

In English, changes in the tenses of the verbs often signal to the reader that the events described are not in chronological (time) order. Such is the case in the selection you just read. Notice, for example, that much of the article is written in the present tense to describe the events as they happen (for example, "As I sip . . ."). In addition, the simple past (for example, "began") and the present perfect (for example, "have landed") are used to refer to events that occurred prior to the eclipse (either at a specific time—simple past—or in the period of time leading up to the eclipse—present perfect).

DIRECTIONS: Following are some of the main events mentioned by Gore, listed in the order in which they appeared in the article. Your task is to put them into the order in which they actually occurred, that is, into chronological order. To do so, use the tenses of the verbs as clues and refer to the article for any additional information you need.

_____ The sounding of the siren ("...a distant siren *could be heard*.")

_____ Wiyono's striking of the Kentongan ("Asmo Wiyono *began to strike*...")

_____ The author's arrival in Java ("I *have come* to Java...")

_____ The landing of machines on the moon, Mars, and Venus ("We, the human race, *have landed*...")

_____ The photography of Jupiter's moons ("We *have braved*... *and photographed*...")

_____ The author's sipping of tea in Wiyono's home ("As I *sip* tea...")

_____ Wiyono listens to his grandmother's story of Betara Kala ("My grandmother and my father *have told* me..." Be careful! Remember that Wiyono is himself a grandfather when he makes this statement.)

_____ The women's singing ("The women in Wiyono's family *begin* to sing...")

_____ An eerie dusk ("An eerie dusk *descends*...")

_____ The appearance of Venus and Mars ("Venus and Mars both *emerge*...")

_____ A mild earthquake ("A mild earthquake *sets* the ground atremble...")

_____ An abrupt sunrise ("an abrupt sunrise *erases* the planets...")

• Comprehending the Meaning: Making Inferences

The literal meaning of an author's words and sentences is actually only a small part of what that author is communicating, for much of his or her meaning is only implied (suggested) rather than stated directly. It is up to you as a reader to make inferences (conclusions, judgments) based on what is stated to understand the author's full meaning and intent.

DIRECTIONS: Use all the information available to you to answer the following questions.

1. The Patuk villagers' feelings about the eclipse could best be described as
     a. fearful.   b. sad.   c. joyful.   d. angry.
    What evidence from the article did you use to infer your answer?

    _____

2. Patuk is
     a. a small village in which life is becoming more modernized.
     b. a traditional village in which people live much the same way as their ancestors did.
     c. a resort town.
     d. a place where a new scientific institute has just been established.

        Your evidence: _____
3. The sentence "I am tempted briefly to believe in giants" (paragraph 7) means:
     a. The author briefly believed the story of Betara Kala.
     b. The author wanted to live in Java and accept that culture.
     c. The author likes to study mythology.
     d. The author was awed by the eclipse.
4. Why does the author use the expressions "untimely evening" and "eerie dusk" in paragraph 7? What feeling do these expressions help to communicate?)

    _____

    _____

    As we studied in unit 2, specific details help you to draw conclusions about the author's meaning. Sometimes, however, the author does not state his or her meaning directly, so the reader must use the information given to make **inferences**.

Becoming a Proficient Writer

Guided Writing: Creating Your Own Myth

Myths are stories told to explain the unknown. Here you will follow a series of steps to create your own myth about a celestial (heavenly) phenomenon.
    Before you begin, think about existing myths with which you are familiar. One myth is described briefly in the reading selection. Like this Indonesian story of the solar eclipse, many myths describe universally apparent events; others seek to explain a phenomenon more specific to a particular location or people. In Hawaii, for example, they tell a story of how the god Maui roped the sun, holding it captive until it agreed to rest for a long period every day over the tropical islands of Hawaii. As a result of Maui's

action, the Hawaiian people had enough light and warmth to grow their crops, and the islands obtained their tropical climate year-round.

● Generating Ideas: Brainstorming With a Group

A. As a class, brainstorm about the myths that your ancestors told about the heavens. As you share these with your classmates, your teacher will list them on the board. As each myth is listed, identify the phenomenon it explains.

Phenomenon	Myth
solar eclipse	Betara Kala eats the sun in revenge for being kicked out of heaven.
tropical climate	Maui ropes the sun to make it shine longer on the islands.

After the class has listed as many myths as it can, go back and discuss the list. Do you see any patterns in the myths? Do most of them involve gods and goddesses (or half-gods) as in the two preceding examples? Do they portray some kind of conflict and resolution to that conflict? What emotions, virtues, or failings are reflected in those conflicts? Did you notice that the myths are all fairly short and simple?

Now that you have examined some of the component parts of a myth, you are ready to break into smaller groups to begin gathering ideas for your own myth.

B. In small groups, choose a heavenly phenomenon that your myth will explain. You may want to choose from the list the class made, or you may want to brainstorm as a group about other possible phenomena before you make your choice. Once your choice is made, brainstorm together about possible characters, their conflict, and its resolution. Assign one student as a secretary to write down all the ideas presented. Then, as a group, review the list and decide on the characters and story line (plot) that you all will use. Each group member should take careful notes on the story that is agreed on, for this will be the basis of what you write.

● Composing

Using the plot and characters your group discussed, write your version of the myth. Remember to keep the story fairly short, but be sure to use the showing techniques you practiced in unit 2. Use changes in the verb tenses if necessary to clarify the sequence of events in the story.

● Sharing Your Myths

After you have each written your version of the myth, reassemble as a group. Read and discuss the various versions. As a group, choose the best version of the myth. Base your choice on how easy it is for the reader to understand the sequence of events and how well the writer used showing details to make the story come alive. Finally, each group should share its best version of their myth with the rest of the class.

LESSON 2

TRAVELERS' TALES

About the Selection:

In this lesson we leave the world of myth and fantasy and enter the world of science, a world in which new technological advances are bringing us closer to solving the mysteries that our ancestors could only dream about. Too often, however, these advances remain technical and understood only by the scientific community. We are fortunate, therefore, that there are scientists like astronomer Carl Sagan who help to spread that knowledge to the general public by writing about it in a comprehensible form. In his book *Cosmos*, Dr. Sagan explores how our knowledge of the universe has expanded over the centuries. "Travelers' Tales," an excerpt from chapter 6 of *Cosmos*, describes one part of humankind's attempt to explore space.

The First Reading

As You Read: Looking for the General Ideas

In this first reading, concentrate on the general ideas. It might help you to think about the following questions.

1. What is Voyager 2?
2. Where did it travel?
3. What aspects of the Voyager 2 mission does this excerpt focus on?

TRAVELERS' TALES
by Carl Sagan

[1]   This is the time when humans have begun to sail the sea of space. The modern ships that ply the Keplerian trajectories[1] to the planets are unmanned. They are beautifully constructed, semi-intelligent robots exploring unknown worlds. Voyages to the outer solar system are controlled from a single place on the planet Earth, the Jet Propulsion Laboratory (JPL) of the National Aeronautics and Space Administration in Pasadena, California.

[2]   On July 9, 1979, a spacecraft called Voyager 2 encountered the Jupiter system. It had been almost two years sailing through interplanetary space. The ship is made of millions of separate parts assembled redundantly, so that if some component fails, others will take over its responsibilities. The spacecraft weighs 0.9 tons and would fill a large living room. Its mission takes it so far from the Sun that it cannot be powered by solar energy, as other spacecraft are. Instead, Voyager relies on a small nuclear power plant, drawing hundreds of watts from the radioactive decay of a pellet of plutonium. Its three integrated computers and most of its housekeeping functions—for example, its temperature-control system—are localized in its middle. It receives commands from Earth and radios its findings back to Earth through a large antenna, 3.7 meters in diameter. Most of its scientific instruments are on a scan platform, which tracks Jupiter or one of its moons as the spacecraft hurtles past. There are many scientific instruments—ultraviolet and infrared spectrometers, devices to measure charged particles and magnetic fields and the radio emission from Jupiter—but the most productive have been the two television cameras, designed to take tens of thousands of pictures of the planetary islands in the outer solar system.

[3]   The Voyager 2 spacecraft will never return to Earth. But its scientific finds, its epic discoveries, its travelers' tales, do return. Take July 9, 1979, for instance. At 8:04 Pacific Standard Time on this morning, the first pictures of a new world, called Europa after an old one, were received on Earth.

[4]   How does a picture from the outer solar system get to us? Sunlight shines on Europa in its orbit around Jupiter and is reflected back to space, where some of it strikes the phosphors of the Voyager televi-

---

[1]**to ply the Keplerian trajectories:** to travel along the curved paths or routes derived from the work of German astronomer Johann Kepler.

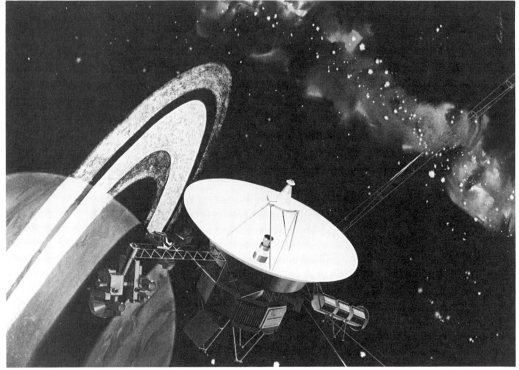

sion cameras, generating an image. The image is read by the Voyager computers, radioed back across the immense intervening distance of half a billion kilometers to a radio telescope, a ground station on the Earth. There is one in Spain, one in the Mojave Desert of Southern California and one in Australia. (On that July morning in 1979 it was the one in Australia that was pointed toward Jupiter and Europa.) It then passes the information via a communications satellite in Earth's orbit to Southern California, where it is transmitted by a set of microwave relay towers to a computer at the Jet Propulsion Laboratory, where it is processed. The picture is fundamentally like a newspaper wirephoto, made of perhaps a million individual dots, each a different shade of gray, so fine and close together that at a distance the constituent dots are invisible. We see only their cumulative effect. The information from the spacecraft specifies how bright or dark each dot is to be. After processing, the dots are then stored on a magnetic disk, something like a phonograph record. There are some eighteen thousand photographs taken in the Jupiter system by Voyager 1 that are stored on such magnetic discs, and an equivalent number for Voyager 2. Finally, the end product of this remarkable set of links and relays is a thin piece of glossy paper, in this case showing the wonders of Europa, recorded, processed and examined for the first time in human history on July 9, 1979.

5   What we saw on such pictures was absolutely astonishing. Voyager 1 obtained excellent imagery of the other three Galilean satellites of Jupiter. But not Europa. It was left for Voyager 2 to acquire the first-close-up pictures of Europa, where we see

things that are only a few kilometers across. At first glance, the place looks like nothing so much as the canal network that Percival Lowell imagined to adorn Mars, and that, we now know from space vehicle exploration, does not exist at all. We see on Europa an amazing, intricate network of intersecting straight and curved lines. Are they ridges—that is, raised? Are they troughs—that is, depressed? How are they made? Are they part of a global tectonic[2] system, produced perhaps by fracturing of an expanding or contracting planet? Are they connected with plate tectonics on the Earth? What light do they shed on the other satellites of the Jovian system? At the moment of discovery, the vaunted technology has produced something astonishing. But it remains for another device, the human brain, to figure it out.

[2]**tectonic:** refers to the results of the movements of the planet's crust, as from earthquakes or faults.

From Carl Sagan, *Cosmos* (Random House) Copyright © 1980 by Carl Sagan. All Rights Reserved. Reprinted by permission of the author.

After You Read

• Identifying the Main Idea

DIRECTIONS: Answer the following questions to check your comprehension of the main ideas presented in the selection.

1. Voyager 2 is
   a. a manned space shuttle.
   b. a complex robot ship controlled from Earth.
   c. a radio telescope with a powerful camera.
2. This article discusses the journey of Voyager 2 toward
   a. Mars.
   b. Saturn.
   c. Jupiter.
3. The "travelers' tales" from Voyager 2 are
   a. photographs and scientific information.
   b. a daily written log kept by the astronauts aboard.
   c. recorded messages from the Voyager 2 crew.

• Guessing Vocabulary From Context

DIRECTIONS: Now that you have a general idea about the selection, it should be easier to predict the meanings of the unfamiliar vocabulary. The following short passages are taken directly from the selection. Use the context given and your knowledge of the article to guess the meanings of the italicized words. Write a synonym or explanation of the word in the space provided.

1. "The ship is made of millions of separate parts assembled *redundantly*, so that if one component fails, others will take over its responsibilities." (Hint: The expression "so that" introduces a purpose.)

   redundantly: _____

2. "[The spacecraft's] mission takes it so far from the sun that it cannot be powered by *solar* energy, as other spacecraft are." (Hint: The expression "so...that" indicates a causal relationship: so + cause + that + result.)

   solar: _____

3. "Instead [of using solar energy], Voyager relies on a small nuclear power plant, drawing hundreds of *watts* from the radioactive decay of a pellet of plutonium."

   watts: _____

4. "The image is... radioed back across the *immense* intervening distance of half a billion kilometers to... Earth." (Hint: "of half a billion kilometers")

   immense: _____

5. "The picture is fundamentally like a newspaper wirephoto, made up of perhaps a million individual dots... so fine and so close together that at a distance the *constituent* dots are invisible. We see only their *cumulative* effect."

   constituent (Hint: Note the expression "so... that."): _____

   _____

   cumulative (Hint: Although the individual dots are invisible at a distance, we can

   still *see* something.): _____

   _____

• Understanding Vocabulary Through Word Analysis

Sometimes, knowing the meanings of parts of the word can also provide clues as to the word's meaning. The following words are derived from the following Latin and Germanic roots and prefixes.

DIRECTIONS: Use both the parts of the words and the context in which they appear to guess their meanings.

Prefixes	Roots
e ....away	mit/mis.............send
ultra ....beyond, excessive	spect.................look at
infra ....below	meter...............measure
inter ....between	ven/vent...........come

1. "There are many scientific instruments—*ultraviolet* and *infrared spectrometers*, devices to measure charged particles and magnetic fields and the radio *emission* from Jupiter—" (paragraph 2)

   ultraviolet: _____

   infrared: _____

   spectrometer: _____

   emission: _____

2. "...radioed back across the immense *intervening* distance... to a radio telescope... on Earth."

   intervening: _____

3. The last two sentences in the selection show the relationship between two factors

   in the Voyager 2 mission. What are they? _____ and _____

   What is their relationship? _____

● Becoming an Efficient Reader: Scanning Prose for Details

In units 1 and 2, you learned to scan charts and graphs to locate specific information. Now you will apply these same techniques to scan a piece of prose.

DIRECTIONS: Answer the following questions. To find the answers quickly, you will need to keep in mind how the article is organized (the author's *plan* as discussed in the previous exercise). Also, be sure to read each question carefully to understand exactly what kind of information you are being asked to find.

1. At what time (exactly) were the first pictures of Jupiter's moon Europa received on Earth?
2. What does JPL stand for? What is its significance?
3. What is the diameter of Voyager 2's antenna?
4. How much does Voyager 2 weigh?
5. How many radio telescopes on Earth receive messages from Voyager 2?
6. How many photographs did Voyager 1 take of the Jupiter system? Where are they stored?
7. Where are the three computers located in Voyager 2?
8. Where are most of the scientific instruments located?

The Second Reading

As You Read: Knowing Your Purpose

This time, concentrate on the author's plan of organization and his choice of supporting details. The following questions should help you.

1. What is the function of the first paragraph? What important information about Voyager 2 does it give?
2. What paragraph describes the Voyager 2 spacecraft? What dominant impression of the spacecraft does it portray?
3. What aspect of the functioning of Voyager 2 is described in detail? Why is this information included? In what order are the details presented?
4. What is the human role in the Voyager 2 mission? Where is it mentioned?

After You Read

● Understanding the Author's Plan

DIRECTIONS: Refer to the reading to answer these questions.

1. Notice that the first paragraph gives some general background information. What two important facts about modern voyages to the planets are mentioned in this paragraph?

    _____

2. The Voyager 2 craft is described in paragraph 2. What is the impression of the spacecraft portrayed in this paragraph?

    _____

3. Paragraph 3 serves as a transition, linking paragraph 2 to the topic of paragraph 4. What significant event does paragraph 3 introduce?

    _____

    How is this event related to the topic of paragraph 4?

    _____

4. What general information is given in paragraph 4? _____

    _____

_____Why do you think Carl Sagan included

this information in detail? _____

Notice that the details in this paragraph are presented in a specific order. In what

kind of order are they presented? _____

Why? _____

• Comprehending a Sequence: Analyzing a Process

Look back over paragraph 4 of the reading selection. What is the purpose of this

paragraph? _____
When we describe *how* a repeated or repeatable goal is accomplished, we say that we are
describing a *process*. A process is made up of a series of steps or actions which, when
performed in sequence, lead to a goal.

DIRECTIONS: Following is a partial list of the steps in the process of transmitting pictures
from Voyager 2 back to Earth. Read paragraph 4 carefully to fill in the
missing steps of the process. Then compare your answers with those of
your classmates.

1. Sunlight shines on Europa.

2. _____

3. _____

4. _____

5. The image is radioed back to a radio telescope on Earth.

6. _____

7. _____

8. The information/image from Voyager 2 is processed at the Jet Propulsion Laboratory.

9. _____

10. _____

Compare your list of steps to the original paragraph. What information in the paragraph does not describe a step (or steps) in the process? Underline it. Why is this extra information included in the paragraph? What does it tell you about the audience (intended readers) for this article?

Now look over your list of steps. What do you notice about the form of the verbs?

What tense is used? _____ Why? _____ Do you

notice any verbs in the passive voice? Which ones?_____
You may want to review the formation and use of the present tense verb forms (simple present, present continuous, and present perfect) and the passive voice since these forms are often used to describe a process.

● Recognizing Sequence Signals

As in a narrative (a story), the sequence of events in a process is very important. To help us understand that sequence clearly, the author usually includes clues or signals of various kinds. In the previous exercise, you probably used some of these clues to identify the steps involved in transmitting photographs back to Earth. In this exercise you'll go back over paragraph 4 to find those sequence clues.

DIRECTIONS: Answer the following questions to help you identify the sequence signals used in paragraph 4.

a. Is an image generated before, after, or at the same time as the light strikes the

phosphors of the Voyager cameras? _____

How do you know this? _____

b. What key word in step 6 indicates that this action occurs *after* the image is radioed

back to earth? _____

c. What key phrase introduces step 9 and indicates that it must come after step 8?

_____

In this exercise, notice how the use of participial phrases (items a and c) transitions (b), and prepositions (c) help to show the reader when the step occurs.

To help you in your writing, we have listed some of the common expressions used to indicate sequence or time relationships. This list is by no means complete, but it will provide you with a beginning repertoire of signals to use in your own writing.

Prepositions (followed by a noun or gerund)	Subordinators (followed by a clause)	Common transitional expressions (used to indicate the relationship between two sentences)	
after	while	then	after that
before	when	finally	by that time
during	after	first, second, etc.	next
	before	meanwhile	later
	until	last	soon
	as		within an hour, day, etc.

Becoming a Proficient Writer

Guided Writing: Using Sequence Signals

This activity will help you to use sequence signals to make your writing clear. It is based on a condition that astronauts must cope with in space, the condition of weightlessness. Because there is no gravity to pull people or objects "downward," even the simplest daily activities become difficult—activities like taking a shower, for instance. How does an astronaut take a shower when there is no gravity to make the water fall "down"? Can you imagine the water droplets continually bouncing around until they finally loose momentum and simply float in the air? To keep the water from floating all over the cabin, scientists have had to develop a collapsible shower stall. The stall is similar to a huge bag which keeps the water enclosed and in control while the astronaut showers.

DIRECTIONS: Listed are the steps (in order) that an astronaut might follow to take a shower in the special collapsible shower stall. Use these steps to write a paragraph instructing new astronauts in the use of the stall. Be sure to include enough signals to make the sequence clear, and use a variety of signals to make it more interesting. You may use the following sentences to begin your paragraph:

From the Astronaut Instruction Manual:
After you have completed your daily exercise, you will, of course, want to refresh yourself with a shower. To do so, you should follow this simple, though somewhat tedious, procedure...

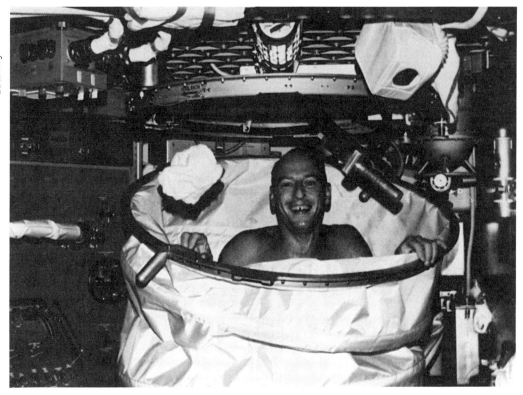

Courtesy of NASA

1. Schedule the shower at a time when you have at least one hour free. (Getting clean in space is a *long* process!)
2. Set up the collapsible shower stall.
3. Remove your clothes and step inside.
4. Close the top of the shower to prevent stray water droplets from escaping into the cabin of the ship.
5. Turn on the water.
6. The water bounces around in the stall.
    Work the soap into a lather.
    Wash your body thoroughly.
7. Use the hand-held vacuum to remove the soapy water.
8. Rinse with fresh water.
9. Vacuum all droplets of water from both the stall and your body.
10. Check to be sure there are no stray droplets floating around.
11. Open the shower stall and step out.
12. Get your clothes and get dressed.
13. Collapse the bag and put it away.
14. Return to your station refreshed but exhausted.

LESSON 3

COMPOSING
ON YOUR OWN

For the main composing activity of this unit, you will write on a topic that involves sequencing.

The First Draft

Choosing a Topic

DIRECTIONS: Choose one of the following topics to write one or two paragraphs about.

A. You have landed on a new planet never before explored by human beings. Write a report back to Earth about your landing and what you saw afterward.
B. Choose a specific task performed regularly in your field of work or study. Explain the process for accomplishing this task in a paragraph addressed to a new worker or student in the field.
C. Select an experience you have had that was of particular significance for you. Describe this experience and its importance in a composition intended for your classmates.

Note: These topics are very different from one another. Topics A and C ask you to tell about an experience, one imaginary and one real. Topic B requires you to explain the steps of a process. Remember that the audience and the purpose of a piece of writing will affect what you write about and how you write it. In making your choice, consider these elements.

Generating Ideas

Topic A: Brainstorm in a group with several other students. What kinds of things would you be likely to notice on a new planet? (Use all five senses.) What tasks would need to be accomplished on that first day? Might you encounter other life forms? Decide what you would do, and list your actions in chronological order. Try to imagine the scene in detail. Describe what you see in a freewriting. Use the looping technique (unit 2) if you wish. (Look for "hot spots" and write about one of them.)

Topic B: You might begin by listing everything you can think of that is related to that process without worrying about the order. Leave spaces to add information later. After you have finished your list, decide what to keep and what to take out, and put everything into its proper time sequence.

Topic C: You might picture the experience first in your mind. Think about where you were, what you were doing, and what was going on around you. When you have a picture in your mind, do a freewriting to describe that experience. Then you might want to use the looping technique (unit 2). Underline "hot spots" in your freewriting and again freewrite on one of them.

Writing the First Draft

Read over the ideas you have generated about your topic. Select the ideas that seem the most interesting and relevant, and write a rough draft of your composition. At this stage, don't worry about grammar and punctuation. Rather, concentrate on getting your ideas down clearly and on developing the sequence of actions relevant to your topic. Remember to include enough showing details for your readers to picture the scene on their own and to draw their own conclusions.

Peerediting for Content

DIRECTIONS: Exchange papers with a partner who is not writing on the same topic as you are. You will read and comment on your partner's paper, and he or she will do the same for yours. Remember that your goal is to help your partner to clarify and develop his or her *ideas*. You should deal with grammatical mistakes only when the errors interfere with your understanding of the author's meaning. Use the following questions as guidelines for discussing the papers with your partner.

1. Read the paper silently from beginning to end. As you read, you might want to mark specific places to come back to when you are discussing the other questions.

2. Tell the writer something you like about the paper. Be specific; show the writer specific sentences you like. This is important because your partner needs to know what is effective and should be kept as well as what needs to be changed.

3. Is the author's purpose for writing this composition clear? If not, make suggestions for how your partner might clarify this purpose.

4. Is the amount and type of information appropriate for the intended reader of this composition? If not, what additions or changes would you suggest?

5. Are there any ideas in the paper that are unclear or confusing to you? Ask any questions you need to in order to understand what the author is trying to say.

6. Is the composition interesting? Point out places where the author could add more details to make the paper more interesting.

Revising

Based on your partner's suggestions and on your new ideas, revise your composition.

The Second Draft

Peerediting for Organization

Now you are ready to write a new draft. This time you need to think about the organization of your paper.

DIRECTIONS: Exchange papers with a partner again for another peerediting session. This time focus on the following questions:

1. Are the ideas presented in a logical order? If not, what changes in the organization would you suggest?

2. Underline any expressions that helped you to follow the sequence of actions in the event or process. Does the writer use enough signals to make the sequence clear? Where should additional or different signals be included?

Writing the Second Draft

Now revise and rewrite based on your ideas and on the feedback your partner gave you. (Note: Several revisions of a composition may be necessary. Don't be discouraged by this; even the best professional writers write, rewrite, and then rewrite again before they are satisfied.)

Proofreading

Once you have finished the final revisions of your paper, it is time to proofread what you have written—that is, to read it again to find and correct any mistakes you have made in sentence structure, grammatical forms, spelling, or punctuation. Proofreading is often a difficult task because it seems that there are so many things to concentrate on at once. To make proofreading easier and more efficient, we suggest that you focus on only one issue at a time, rather than on everything all at once.

DIRECTIONS: First, reread your paper for areas that sound wrong. Then, make your more specific goal to correct mistakes in verb form and tenses. As you go through the paper, put your pencil on each verb and ask yourself:

1. Is the verb tense appropriate for the ideas and the sequence I am trying to communicate?
2. Is the verb formed correctly? (Does it agree in number with its subject? Do I have the correct past tense form or participle for the verb?)

Sharing Your Writing

After your teacher has read all the compositions, he or she may decide to share a few with the class so that you can see what your fellow students have done with the topics. Use this opportunity productively. Look for parts of the compositions that are particularly effective or interesting. How did the writer develop these points? Are there any new techniques used that you could apply to your writing?

Keeping a Journal

Choose an idea from the readings, the discussions, or your freewritings that interests you and that you would like to explore further. Develop this idea in more depth in your journal. The following are some example topics:

1. Do you think there is life on other planets? If so, describe what you think alien life forms might be like. If not, explain your reasons for believing there is no life on other planets.
2. Imagine that you will soon travel as a settler to a new planet colony. What items from Earth would you choose to take with you, and why?

UNIT FOUR

IN THE ARENA: SPORTS AND RECREATION

LESSON 1

RUNNING FOR WOMEN

About the Selection:

Like all other aspects of our lives, the field of sports and recreation is constantly changing. Technological advances have affected the professional and competitive athletic world. At the same time, complex social factors have altered the leisure time of a broad spectrum of society. One such broadly felt change is the mushrooming popularity of aerobic sports in general and of long-distance running in particular. The following selection is the introduction to the book *Running for Women*. In it, author-runner Janet Heinonen discusses this new running movement, addressing herself to a very particular segment of the population.

Before You Read: Considering the Audience

Consider the source of this selection (the author and the book title); then look at the picture accompanying it. Who do you think is the intended audience for this reading?

In unit 1, you saw how your own writing changed both in **content** (what information you included and why) and in **form** (how you expressed that information) depending on your chosen audience. Now consider your answer to the preceding question. Would you expect the intended audience in this case to affect the author's choice of what to say and how to say it?

_____ If so, why or in what ways? _____

_____

As You Read: Recognizing Audience and Purpose

Keep in mind the intended audience for this selection and think about the following questions.

1. What elements have been included in this passage to appeal specifically to Heinonen's chosen audience?
2. What elements might be equally relevant to a more general audience?
3. What do you think is the author's purpose in writing this introduction?

RUNNING FOR WOMEN
by Janet Heinonen

1   Why run?

2   Some reasons are obvious. It's simple; it's healthy; it is also becoming a national pastime. If you are a woman who gave up sports when she discovered boys, lost her child's figure, or was told by her mother to "act like a lady," you will find an easy and attractive way to explore the realm of athletics you may have missed because you were born female in a male-oriented sports world.

3   You can dabble in running, using it strictly as a conditioner for other athletic activities. You can be more disciplined and use it to achieve the fitness you had long ago forsaken. Running can introduce you to the competitive side of your nature. You can even approach the sport with the seriousness of an Olympian and call yourself "athlete"—deservedly.

4   Or you can run for the fun of it. Whether you prefer solitary runs, where the mind wanders from the pressures and demands of the day, or companionable runs with friends, running can be a relaxing yet invigorating part of every day.

5   Not too many years ago my mother jogged in the alley behind our house because she was embarrassed to be seen jogging in public. Now thousands of women my mother's age, older, and younger are taking to the streets, parks, and tracks confident enough to give the world a run for its money, undaunted by the would-be heckler. Fortunately, as the ranks of women runners swell, the hecklers are disappearing. Even they can't quarrel with numbers.

6   And women are running. They came on 4300 strong in the 1978 Women's Central Park Mini-Marathon race (10,000 meters) in New York City. Six hundred women ran in the 26.2-mile Honolulu Marathon the year before. In the spring of 1978, some 250 women entered the Boston Marathon, with its strict qualifying time of 3 hours, 30 minutes for women—26 miles at an 8-minutes-per-mile pace. Several years ago, the thought of an eight-minute mile would have elicited a "Who, me? You've got to be kidding!" from many of these same women. For that matter, several years ago the thought of legions of women choosing

an alternative to the sedentary life and re-capturing the fitness and vigor of their youth might have seemed strange to anyone.

7   Running is easy.

8   You don't have to be athletic to be a runner. For the woman who despairs at the thought of trying to master a passable tennis game, who trips on her feet playing racquetball, or who can't keep her balance on a bicycle, running is easy. You may not look like Wilma Rudolph when you start out, but the important thing is not *how* you run, it's that you *do* run.

9   You can approach running from any angle. Most women start running to lose weight or to become fit. Many continue running for those reasons, while others, in increasing numbers, find themselves edging into the world of competitive running. Many women "fun runners" are suddenly finding themselves at the head of the field in road races. Some, especially women with an athletic background, start

Larry Fleming

running with the express purpose of competing. Others—like many men—may
have run competitively at one time and
find that they instinctively keep on running, whether they're competing or not.

10   Running is inexpensive. Outside of a
good pair of shoes... you're not gong to
need any special equipment. Or lessons.
Or facilities.

11   One of the joys of running is being
able to tie your house key to your shoelaces
and head off on a run, unencumbered. No
purse or pack to carry. No car to park. No
equipment to grip. You're off and running
free.

12   The world is your course. You can
run around the block, at your local outdoor
or indoor track, on country roads, in city
parks, on mountain trails, through down-
town streets, or in your high school hall-
ways. Some people have even measured
out running courses inside their homes.

13   It takes bravery and a thick skin to
take to the street, putting yourself on dis-
play. But keep your chin up and ignore
those flabby fools who cruise by in cars,
giving you grief. Answer their leers with
insufferable forgiveness. Remember:
You're better than they are.

From Sports Illustrated *Running for Women: A Complete Guide* by Janet Heinonen, published by Sports Illustrated Winner's Circle Books. Copyright © 1989 by Time Inc.

After You Read

● Guessing Vocabulary from Context

DIRECTIONS: Several short excerpts from the reading selection follow. Use the contextual clues to guess the meaning of the italicized words in each excerpt.
Write your guess (a synonym or general explanation of the word) in the
space provided.

1. "You can *dabble* in running, using it strictly as a conditioner for other activities. You
can be more disciplined and use it to achieve the fitness you had long ago forsaken."
(Hint: What does the use of "more disciplined" in the second sentence indicate
about the amount of seriousness or discipline implied by the verb *dabble*?)

dabble:_____

2. "...running can be a relaxing yet *invigorating* part of every day."
(Hint: Notice that the coordinator "yet" indicates a contrast in meaning between the
words *relaxing* and *invigorating*. Notice also the use of the root noun *vigor* at the end
of paragraph 6: ...recapturing the fitness and vigor of their youth...")

invigorating:_____

3. "Now thousands of women... are taking to the streets, parks, and tracks confident
enough to give the world a run for its money, *undaunted* by the would-be heckler."
(Hint: The use of the comma to set off the final phrase of the sentence indicates a

close relationship between the adjectives *confident* and *undaunted*. A heckler is someone who tries to bother or interrupt another person by making threatening or insulting remarks.)

undaunted:_____

4. "Several years ago, the thought of an eight-minute mile would have elicited a 'Who, me? You've got to be kidding!' from many of these same women. For that matter, several years ago, the thought of legions of women choosing an alternative to the *sedentary* life... might have seemed strange to anyone."

(Hint: Notice the parallel structure in these two sentences; that is, "Several years ago, the thought of ... Several years ago, the thought of..." This parallelism indicates a close relationship between running an eight-minute mile and "choosing an alternative to the sedentary life." What lifestyle is running an *alternative* to?)

sedentary:_____

5. "One of the joys of running is being able to tie your house key to your shoelaces and head off on a run, *unencumbered*. No purse or pack to carry. No car to park. No equipment to grip. You're off and running free."

(Hint: Notice the repetition of the word *no*.)

unencumbered:_____

● Identifying the Author's Purpose

Notice that the author refers directly to the reader throughout the selection.

What pronoun does she use to refer to the reader? _____

In paragraph 2, Heinonen gives an indication of why she is writing to this particular

audience. What word does she use to characterize the sports world? _____

What do you think this word means? _____

Given her characterization of the sports world, does the author believe it is general-

ly easy or difficult for a woman to participate in sports? _____

DIRECTIONS: Use the preceding answers as clues to help you decide which of the following best represents the author's purpose in her introduction:

a.   to explain the health benefits of running
b.   to interest women in competitive running

c. to explain why running has become popular among women
d. to encourage women to take up the sport of running

You can see how the author's purpose, as well as her audience, has shaped this passage. Her use of the pronoun *you*, her persuasive and positive style, and even her angry reference to "flabby fools who cruise by in cars" are determined by her purpose, to convince women that running is a wonderful thing to do.

● Recognizing the Author's Plan

Notice that the selection is organized into three main sections, as indicated by the extra space between them. Notice also that each of these sections emphasizes a particular area. The answers to the following questions will help you to identify the focus on each section and thus to see the author's overall plan of development.

1. Which section stresses the growing acceptance of women runners?
2. Which section focuses on the benefits women can gain from running?
3. Which section emphasizes how easy it is to take up running?

DIRECTIONS: Now restate briefly the main idea of each section; then find the principal supporting points for each and write them in the space provided.

SECTION 1:

Main idea: _____

Supporting points: _____

_____

_____

SECTION 2:

Main idea: _____

Supporting points: _____

_____

SECTION 3:

Main idea: _____

_____

Supporting points: _____

_____

_____

_____

_____

Conclusion: _____

Becoming a Proficient Writer

Writing to an Audience

DIRECTIONS: For this exercise you should work in small groups. Follow the steps listed to understand more fully how an author writes to a specific audience.

1. Compare your list of main ideas and supporting points with those of the other members of your group. Try to reach an agreement on what these points should be.
2. Go back over your lists, referring as needed to the reading section.
    a. Decide which of the author's points are relevant *only* to her women readers.
    b. Which of the points receive special emphasis or wording because of the female audience?
    c. Which points would be equally relevant to the would-be male runner as to the would-be female runner?
3. Imagine that your group is to rewrite this piece for a male readership. In each section, decide what you would omit, what you would change, and what you would add to make the selection more relevant to a male audience. To make these decisions, you'll need to consider the sports experience of the average man and the reasons he might have to begin running. (Note: For this exercise, you need not actually *rewrite* the selection. Simply make the preliminary decisions as though you were rewriting it.)
4. When you have finished, compare your group's answers with those of the other groups. Did you make similar changes? Why or why not?

As you saw in the guided writing in unit 1, audience will determine both *what* we choose to write and *how* we choose to write it.

Generating Ideas: Practicing Your Techniques

In the first three units, you learned several techniques to help you develop your ideas for writing. In this exercise you will practice three of these: brainstorming, free-writing, and looping. This activity will help you to discover which techniques work best for you. As you become more experienced with these and other methods, you will become a better judge of which you prefer to use and how you prefer to use them.

● Brainstorming

Close your eyes for a moment. Imagine yourself with a free afternoon or weekend. What will you do? Swim? Play soccer? Read a book? Play some music? Think of your alternatives. Then make a list of all the sports and other recreational activities you enjoy.

● Freewriting

When you have finished your list, choose one activity to write about. It should be something that you enjoy doing and could recommend to others to try. At the top of a clean sheet of paper, write "Why _____?" Fill in the blank with the name of the activity you have chosen.

Now, write for seven to ten minutes in response to the question you have just written.

● Looping

Read over your freewriting. Underline any points you find particularly interesting and would like to develop further. Choose one of these and do a second freewriting (your first "loop") for seven to ten minutes.

Follow the same procedure with your "loop" that you did with the first freewriting: Underline the "hot spots" of interest. Then choose one of these (or one from the first freewriting) and write again for seven to ten minutes.

Save your freewriting and loops in your idea notebook, as you may want to develop them further in lesson 2.

LESSON 2

ULTRA SPORTS

About the Selection:

Have you ever noticed how in recent years major sports records are frequently broken and reestablished only to be broken again a short time later? Whereas achievements like the four-minute mile, the seven-foot high jump, or the sixteen-foot pole vault stood for decades as lofty goals that no athlete was able to reach, these former barriers are today surpassed with great regularity. What can account for this rise in athletic achievement? Why do athletes today seem to run faster, jump higher, and throw farther than those of just twenty or thirty years ago? In this article for *Omni* magazine, Mark Teich and Pamela Weintraub explore important changes taking place in the world of sports, changes that both help to explain some of the new accomplishments and promise even greater achievements in the years to come.

The First Reading

Before You Read: Anticipating the Topic

1. Read the full title of this article (page 83). *Lab* is a short form of the word *laboratory*. What usually takes place in a laboratory? _____ What do you think is meant by "Out of the lab and into the stadium"? _____ Do you expect this article to discuss the sports activities of the average individual or of training athletes? _____

2. Now look at the graphics and read the captions. Do these seem to confirm the predictions you made from the title? _____ State briefly, but as specifically as possible, what you expect this article to discuss. _____

3. Now consider the audience. This article was written for *Omni*, a popular science magazine in the U.S. Do you expect the intended audience of this article to be more *specific* or more *general* than the intended audience of the reading selection in lesson 1? _____ For what type of reader do you think this article was written? _____

As You Read: Attacking a Longer Reading

As you flipped through the pages to look at the graphics, you probably noticed that this article is considerably longer than previous readings in this text. Now that you have practiced some of the basic reading skills and strategies, you are ready to begin tackling longer readings. One useful method for doing this is to look for the author's plan of organization as you read. This approach helps you to see which ideas are related to one another and how the author is building his or her argument or analysis.

Usually a longer reading can be broken into several shorter sections, each of which has a particular focus. Sometimes the author will indicate these sections by placing breaks or subtitles between them, as in the first reading of this unit. Often, however, you must discover the sections yourself. By continually asking yourself what will come next and looking for any signals the author gives you, you will be able to recognize and anticipate changes in focus as they occur.

DIRECTIONS: This first reading is intended to give you a general understanding of the article and a sense of the focus of each section. Although the vocabulary in this article is rather sophisticated, don't worry at this time about the words you don't know. Vocabulary exercises will follow the first reading. To give you practice in recognizing the author's plan and anticipating the text, we have included prediction questions at key points in the article. When you come to these questions, choose the appropriate response.

OUT OF THE LAB
AND INTO THE STADIUM:
ULTRA SPORTS
By Mark Teich and Pamela Weintraub

1   Even practicing on the track. Edwin Moses runs with rhythmic precision, taking one identical stride after the next. On every thirteenth step, approaching each new hurdle,[1] he initiates a complicated series of movements. All in one beat, he gracefully bends his back, tucks his head toward his knees, and points one arm straight ahead for balance. Suddenly he is airborne. Lead leg thrust out like a saber, he seems momentarily frozen in space, an icon[2] of the athlete's eternal quest for perfection.

2   Moses has come closer to perfection than any athlete in history. A two-time Olympic gold medal-winner in the 400-meter intermediate hurdles, he has set new world records on four separate occasions. Undefeated in his event for the past eight years, he has sprinted to victory *109 times in a row*. No other runner has ever done so well in a single race so often.

3   But if you ask the top track and field experts in the country, they will say that Moses is neither the fastest 400-meter runner, nor the best pure hurdler. What he is,

though, is the world's greatest student of his event. A National Merit Scholar educated in physics and civil engineering, Moses continually analyzes his performance with the latest tools of modern technology.

4   Early and late in each season, he tests himself on weight machines that give a computerized readout of his strength and power in different body regions; at a glance, he can see whether he has muscle imbalances that may slow his speed or even threaten injury. He has worked with a team of technicians and engineers to take high-speed videotapes during training, then studied the tape frame[3] by frame to locate any flaws in his technique. And during his most grueling[4] workouts, he wears a heart monitor that records his pulse rate every 30 seconds and relays it to a computer memory in his wristwatch. Hours later, he records the pulse measurements and practice times on a home computer.

5   But despite Moses's reliance on technology, fellow athletes don't consider him a

[1]**hurdle:** a barrier over which the runner must leap
[2]**icon:** image, picture
[3]**frame:** each separate picture on a strip of film
[4]**grueling:** exhausting

maniac.[5] Far from being an anomaly in sports, he is a respected pioneer. Like the protohumans who carried the first blunt clubs into battle or the hunter-gatherers who sent the first wheel down a hill, he is a harbinger of things to come.

Prediction: The previous paragraph characterizes Moses as "a respected pioneer... a harbinger of things to come." Based on this and on your earlier predictions about the topic of this article, what do you expect the next section of the article to do?

   a. analyze Edwin Moses's career in greater detail.

   b. proceed to a more general discussion of the growing use of technology in sports.

---

6   With each passing year, the once straightforward (throw it fast, hit it hard) world of athletics is becoming increasingly complex. To survive, competitors like Moses are resorting to strategies continually developed in research labs and on the playing field itself. Working hand in hand with physicists, physiologists, and psychologists, they are forging the techniques that will revolutionize athletics in the twenty-first century.

7   When this revolution has peaked, human performance will enter a superhuman realm. The future athlete will move faster, jump higher, hit harder, and compete with far more skill. This quantum leap will be propelled by such scientific tools as:

• Computer programs that analyze the motion of every limb[6] and muscle, suggesting how the athlete can alter his or her movements for optimal performance.

• An extensive series of diagnostic tests to identify future world-class athletes and de-termine the best sport for each individual.

• Electrodes that literally program an athlete's muscles with electrical signals taken from superstars.

• Biofeedback devices that measure physiological features from heartbeats to brainwaves, helping the athlete to fine-tune performance from moment to moment during a game or event.

8   These possibilities are natural outgrowths of research that has gathered momentum for more than 20 years. The spiritual father of high-tech sports, Israeli Gideon Ariel, got the ball rolling (so to speak) shortly after the 1964 Tokyo Olympics.

Prediction: Did you notice the shift in focus in paragraph 8? Based on this shift, what do you expect the next section to do?

   a. review the work of Gideon Ariel and the history of "high tech sports"

   b. continue to discuss future possibilities

---

9   Ariel understood that the laws of nature were not truly accessible to the human eye. To compensate for the eye's deficiencies, he began to film athletes with high-speed cameras. Then he took the film and manually calculated the motion of limbs and other body segments frame by frame. Using the laws of Newtonian physics to measure performance, he discovered an astounding fact: Even superstars made moves that were wasteful or completely wrong. Moreover, when they modified their movements to conform to Ariel's analysis, their performances invariably improved.

10   But this new "biomechanical" approach (in which the body was treated

---

[5]**maniac:** madman; insane person
[6]**limb:** arm or leg

 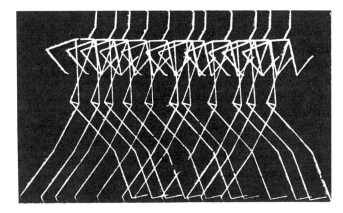

Stick-figure runners generated by computer of high-tech trainer Gideon Ariel. The figure of a runner is digitally copied into a compuer and reproduced to analyze the runner's style.

like a mechanical system) still had limitations. Because the mathematical formulations were so complex, Ariel could work with only a small number of athletes. And he certainly couldn't analyze the *dozens* of body segments that come into play.

11 Then, in 1968, Ariel discovered the computer. He could film athletes, then *automatically* enter their subtlest motions into the computer. Once the data were entered, Ariel's program could create stick figures of an athlete in motion. By modifying the figures to test different positions and speeds, Ariel would finally arrive at an optimal model whose mechanics would lead to the best performance.

12 It didn't take long before Ariel was recruited by the United States Olympic Committee (USOC) at its new headquarters, in Squaw Valley, California. By the early Eighties, he was able to film athletes at the speed of 10,000 frames per second and project the image onto a screen containing 20,000 ultrasensitive microphones. The information could be converted to three-dimensional images of athletes traveling through their entire range of motion. Each image could be frozen at any point or from any perspective for observation.

Prediction: The previous section has reviewed Ariel's pioneering work from 1964 to his "discovery" of the computer in 1968 to his high-speed filming of athletes in the early 1980s. Given this *chronological* progression, what do you expect the next section to do?

a. describe Ariel's background and personal career

b. discuss the state of Ariel's "biomechanical approach" today and predictions for the future

13 As might be expected, the [U.S.] Olympic biomechanics lab [today] is a sort of technological arcade. Wherever you look, computers dominate. In one area of the room, embedded in the floor, are a set of one-and-a-half-foot-long electronic sheets called force plates. As an athlete goes through the motions of his sport, a computer records forces moving forward, backward, up, down, and side to side. In another corner, competitors attach 14 tiny sensors to the soles of their feet. Wires carry data from the sensors to small computers worn by the athletes.

14 Perhaps the most important new de-

velopment in the lab, says researcher Gary Scierman, is the use of computers to visually depict the biomechanics of movement in *real time*—as it occurs. A system known as Selspot, for instance, employs an infrared camera which feeds an image directly into the computer.

15   Videotape, another important tool, can't yet capture as much detail as film. But Schierman notes that it can be played back immediately without waiting to be developed. And like the signals from [Selspot], video signals can be fed directly into the computer. This allows athletes to correct errors in seconds instead of waiting days for film.

16   According to Chuck Dillman, head of biomechanics and sports science at Colorado Springs, this new technology was one reason for America's recent avalanche of Olympic silver and gold.

17   But even these programs, says Dillman, will be kid stuff compared with the *next* generation of software—a *universal* sports program being developed at the lab. "The goal for 1992," he explains, "is a generalized human model that will do biomechanical analysis for *any* sport. We'll be able to modify it quickly for each individual athlete. Instead of three body segments, it will analyze nineteen segments through the entire range of motion. And it will analyze the forces exerted by specific muscles as well."

18   Biomechanical analysis will become increasingly more sophisticated as scientists learn more about the body itself. "Right now we can tell athletes how much they weigh and how much body fat they have," says USOC physiologist Peter Van Handel. "But soon we'll be able to determine optimal patterns of heartbeats, aerobic capacity, metabolism and innumerable blood variables for each athlete in every sport."

19   This wealth of physiological knowledge, says Van Handel, will immeasurably improve the nurturing[7] of athletes from the beginning to the end of their careers. And in the near future, each athlete may be able to scientifically select the best sport for his or her body before ever setting foot on the athletic field.

20   Then, through the partnership of medical science and computer technology, precision training [like that of Edwin Moses] will help bring these future athletes to the very limit of their natural potential.

Prediction: Consider what has been discussed so far in the article and observe now much of the article remains. What do you expect the next section to do?

    a. conclude the article by tying together what has already been discussed

    b. raise a new topic for analysis and discussion

---

21   It seems clear that today's scientists are already redefining the criteria for academic excellence. Dr. Kenneth Cooper, father of the American aerobics revolution, believes that all of the most cherished world records will soon be demolished. "We'll see things like a sub-two-hour marathon and a sub-three-minute forty-second mile in perhaps twenty years," he says.

22   The more impressive the accomplishments, though, the more insistent certain questions may become. For example, as sports tend to become a 50-50 partnership between scientists and competitors, will athletes be sacrificing their personal freedom? And as they become more dependent on science, will they still be *athletes* in the original sense of the word, or will they simply be receptacles[8] for technology?

---

[7]**nurturing:** the training; the care of
[8]**receptacle:** container

23   Ken Cooper, for one, sees these as real concerns. "I'd hate to see all of this go *too* far, until the Olympics become nothing but a year-2050 space-age war between countries trying to prove their technical superiority," he says.

24   But surgeon and former head of the USOC Sports Medicine Council, Dr. Irving Dardick, has no such worries. "We have simply evolved," he says. "Today science and technology are part of us. How can we divorce science from athletics when we don't divorce it from anything else in life?"

25   The real question, Dardick contends, is not *whether* we should use science in sports, but rather, *how*. "There's a tremendous order in the universe, a pattern, and if we want to command the potential of nature, it's a pattern we'll have to understand," Dardick says. "We have to take that pattern and make it useful to the athlete."

26   The key word in Dardick's vision, Moses would agree, is *useful*. The athlete is still the irreducible force, and he must use technology only as it serves his needs. "You can't use science to manufacture an athlete," Moses says. "Raw talent still beats mass production. My scientific approach is not imposed on me. It's completely natural; it just makes it easier to accomplish what I do."

After You Read

• Discovering the Main Idea

DIRECTIONS: Choose the statement that best represents the main idea of the passage.

a. Edwin Moses is a pioneer in applying science to improve sports performance.

b. Computer analysis can help an athlete predict which sport is best suited for his or her body.

c. Some observers argue that athletes who rely on technology may be sacrificing their freedom and the true spirit of athletic competition.

d. Today's athletes and scientists are developing new scientific and technological tools which will greatly change the future of athletic competition.

• Guessing Vocabulary from Context

DIRECTIONS: The following sentences are based on the reading selection *Ultra Sports*. Use the context provided to guess the meaning of the word in italics. Underline the clues you used to make your guess, and write a synonym or explanation of the word in the space provided.

1. Edwin Moses runs with rhythmic precision, taking one identical *stride* after the other.

    stride: _____

2. Moses seems momentarily frozen in space, an image of the athlete's *quest* for eternal perfection.

    quest: _____

3. Moses has *sprinted* to victory 109 times in a row. No other runner has ever done so well in a single race so often.

    sprinted: _____

4. Moses has worked with a team of technicians and engineers to take high-speed videotapes during training, then studied the tape to locate any *flaws* in his technique.
    (Hint: If Moses is always trying to improve his technique, what will he be looking for in the tapes?)

    flaws: _____

5. But despite Moses's reliance on technology, fellow athletes don't consider him a madman. Far from being an *anomaly* in sports, he is a respected pioneer.
    (Hint: The expression "Far from being a..." indicates that Moses is *not* an anomaly, but a pioneer instead.)

    anomaly: _____

6. Like the protohumans who carried the first blunt clubs into battle or the hunter-gatherers who sent the first wheel down a hill, he is a *harbinger* of things to come.
    (Hint: Notice the key words *like, first,* and *things to come.*)

    harbinger: _____

7. Working hand in hand with physicists, physiologists, and psychologists, sports competitors are *forging* the techniques that will revolutionize athletics in the twenty-first century.

    forging: _____

8. When that revolution has peaked, human performance will enter a superhuman realm. The future athlete will move faster, jump higher, hit harder, and compete with far more skill. This *quantum leap* will be propelled by such tools as...
    (Hint: Notice the demonstrative adjective *this.* To what does it refer?)

    quantum leap: _____

9. Often an author will use key words repeatedly in a particular piece of writing. By noticing the context in which a word appears each time, you can often guess more accurately the meaning of that word. Such is the case with the words *modify* and *optimal* in this reading.

   ...suggesting how the athlete can alter his or her movements for *optimal* performance.

   When the athletes *modified* their performance to conform to Ariel's analysis, their performances improved.

   By *modifying* the figures to test different positions and speeds, Ariel would finally arrive at an *optimal* model whose mechanics would lead to the best performance.

   Soon we'll be able to determine *optimal* patterns of heartbeats, aerobic capacity, and so on for each athlete in every sport.

   modify: _____

   optimal: _____

The Second Reading

As You Read: Recognizing the Author's Plan

Check the predictions you made during the first reading and look again for the author's plan. The following questions should help you.

1. How and why is the example of Edwin Moses used?
2. What is the focus of each section, and how is it related to the overall development of the article?
3. What issues are raised at the end of the article? Why?

After You Read

● Using the Author's Plan to Comprehend the Meaning

DIRECTIONS: The following questions are divided into two columns. Those on the left refer to the authors' overall plan of organization and ask you to select the appropriate purpose of each section of the article. Answer these purpose questions for each section. Then answer the more detailed comprehension questions to the right.

Authors' Plan

Section 1 (paragraphs 1–5)
The purpose of this section is
a. to interest the reader in the topic by using a specific example.

Comprehension Questions

1. In what sport does Edwin Moses partici-

   pate? _____

b. to praise Edwin Moses for his success.

c. to inform the reader about a great athlete.

2. What evidence do the authors include to show that Moses is an outstanding athlete? _____

_____

_____

3. Why is Edwin Moses respected as a pioneer in sports? _____

_____

Section 2 (paragraphs 6–8)

The main purpose of this section is

a. to explain a specific point from the first section.

b. to introduce a new supporting point.

c. to state and explain the main idea of the article.

4. In what paragraph is the main idea of the article stated? _____

In what sentence of the paragraph? ____

5. In your own words, write the main idea of the article. _____

_____

_____

6. The computer programs, diagnostic tests, electrodes, and biofeedback devices mentioned in paragraph 7 are all examples of _____.

Section 3 (paragraphs 9–12)

The purpose of this section is

a. to introduce another great athlete.

7. Who is Gideon Ariel? _____

_____

b. to provide historical background on the new "high-tech sports" phenomenon.

c. to analyze one of the tools mentioned in the previous section.

Why does this section focus on his work?

_____

8. What is the "biomechanical approach"?

_____

_____

9. Why was Ariel's "discovery" of the computer a significant development in this field? _____

_____

_____

_____

Section 4 (paragraphs 13—20)

The purpose of this section is

a. to describe some of the scientific tools and information which are revolutionizing competitive sports.

b. to describe in detail the U.S. Olympic Committee biomechanics lab.

10. What tool "dominates" in the Olympic biomechanics lab? _____

What is meant by the term *dominates* in this case? _____

11. What are the advantages of videotape?

_____

_____

12. What is the purpose of the universal sports program mentioned by Dillman?

_____

Has it been developed yet? _____

13. Paragraphs 13–17 focus on the technological tools being developed in this field. What is the general focus of paragraphs 18–20?_____

_____

Section 5 (paragaphs 21–26)

The purpose of section 5 is to conclude the article. To accomplish this goal, the authors

a. introduce a new point for analysis.
b. summarize the main points of the article.
c. raise questions about the trend toward high-tech sports.

14. Why do you think Ken Cooper predicts that all of today's sports records will soon be broken? _____

_____

Based on your reading of the article, would you agree with this prediction?

15. Does Irving Dardick believe that we should continue to use science to improve sports performance? _____

Why? _____

_____

Notice how the combined purposes of the sections establish an overall purpose for the article.

• Taking a Deeper Look: Questions for Discussion

1. The authors call Edwin Moses the "greatest student of his event." Do you think that Moses' scientific knowledge makes him a better *athlete* "in the original sense of the word"?

2. This article focuses on the use of technology to improve an athlete's performance. Some scientists and performers are also experimenting with the use of drugs and hormones to accomplish this same goal. Do you think athletes should be allowed to use drugs in international competition? Why or why not?

LESSON 3

COMPOSING
ON YOUR OWN

In the first two lessons you read about some recent developments in the field of sports. Now you will write a composition of your own about this field.

The First Draft

Choosing a Topic

DIRECTIONS: Choose one of the following topics for a composition three to four paragraphs long.

A. Choose a sport or recreational activity you enjoy. If you don't enjoy sports, try another hobby like handicrafts, painting, or music. Write a composition on the benefits of this activity. Your audience for this composition is anyone who might be interested in participating in this activity, and your purpose is to convince them to do so.

B. Consider this question:

Will the use of science and technology to improve athletic performance be mainly beneficial (good, helpful) or mainly detrimental (bad, harmful) to international sports competition?

Write a composition stating your opinion and the reasons for that opinion. Your audience for this composition is that section of the general public that is interested in sports, and your purpose is to convince them of your opinion.

Generating Ideas

Topic A: You might want to use the brainstorming and freewriting activities you did in lesson 1 as the basis for this composition. You can continue with these same techniques in any combination or order that you wish. Perhaps you have developed your own techniques. Use what works best for you.

Topic B: One way to begin is to brainstorm with your classmates about possible advantages and disadvantages to the use of technology in sports. Then use any other idea-generating techniques that are productive for you.

Writing the First Draft

Use the thoughts you have generated to write your first draft. At this stage, concentrate on keeping your ideas open, considering audience and purpose, and including points that are well supported by details.

Peerediting for Content

DIRECTIONS: Exchange papers with a classmate who has written on a different topic from yours. You will peeredit your partner's paper as you did in unit 3. Keep in mind that you are looking at the expression and development of the *ideas* in the paper, not yet at the organization or the grammar and mechanics. You might want to answer the following questions about your partner's composition on a separate sheet of paper. Then discuss each of the points with him or her after you have finished.

1. What is the main idea of the composition? Is it clearly stated? Where?
2. What are the principal supporting points? (For topic A, these would be the main benefits to be gained from the sport or activity. For topic B, they would be the main reasons for your partner's position on the issue.)
3. Are the supporting points clearly stated? Where?
4. Are there enough details, facts, examples, or other supporting evidence to support the principal points? If not, which points need more development? Can you make any suggestions for how the author might improve these points?

Revising

Consider your peerreader's comments, and make the revisions that you think are necessary. Then consider the following section on organizational concerns.

The Second Draft

As you develop the second draft of your composition, the main focus will be on organizing your ideas to communicate them more effectively. One aspect of organizing your ideas is to begin with a good introduction.

Interesting Your Reader: The Introduction

Quickly look back over the first six paragraphs of *Ultra Sports*. How did the authors

get you involved in the topic of the article? _____
Why do you think they chose to describe Edwin Moses instead of some other athlete to

begin this article? _____
This section of the reading serves as an introduction.

Notice how the introduction progresses: first the authors show you a picture of Moses running through his event; then they describe his training method, which is directly connected to the topic of the article. Finally, in paragraphs 5 and 6, they tie the example of Edwin Moses to the topic and point of the article as a whole. This progression from a specific example or examples to a more general topic is one common way of engaging the reader in a piece of writing. Some other popular techniques are to:

1. Provide general background or historical information and then move to the more specific topic at hand. See, for example, "The World's Urban Explosion," unit 2.
2. Describe a particular incident. The first reading selection in unit 2 is actually the introduction to *The Population Bomb*. Notice how Erlich uses the incident in Delhi to engage the reader in the topic of overpopulation.
3. Use a contrast; that is, begin with one way of looking at a topic and then move to a contrasting approach that will provide the basis for the remainder of the composition. Look back, for example, at the first selection in unit 3. This reading is, again, the introduction to a much longer article, "The Planets: Between Fire and Ice." In it, Gore contrasts the ancient and mythical view of the heavens with a more modern and scientific analysis.
4. Begin with a quotation by a famous individual or expert in the field. Notice the quotation by Toffler at the beginning of unit 1, lesson 1, for example.

These are only a few of the possible techniques. Probably any one of them could have been used in the introduction to *Ultra Sports*. The choice of which technique to use and what information to include will, of course, depend on the intended reader. If the introduction is not *relevant to the reader*, then it will not fulfill one of its two main functions: to interest the person in reading the entire article.

Not only must an introduction be relevant to the reader; it must also be *relevant to the topic* under discussion, for it introduces that topic to the reader. The authors of *Ultra Sports* undoubtedly chose to describe Moses because he uses many of the techniques discussed in the article and has, in fact, participated in their development. Thus, the introduction serves its second main function: to introduce the topic of the composition.

Writing Your Own Introduction

Now you will write an introduction to your composition on sports. Don't worry about making your introduction perfect or about finding the one "right" approach. There is no single right approach, so relax and experiment a little. You'll probably enjoy it more if you do.

DIRECTIONS: Read over the draft that you have written. How did you begin your composition?

If you already included an introduction, consider the following:

1. What technique(s) did you use?
2. Could you have used a different technique?
3. Which one or ones?
4. Try writing an alternate introduction using a different technique.
5. Choose the one you like better.

If you did not include an introduction in your draft, you will write one now.

1. Consider which techniques might be appropriate for your reader and your purpose.
2. Write an introduction using one of these techniques.
3. Try writing one or two different introductions.
4. Choose the one you like the best.

Note: Many authors typically write their introduction after they have prepared a draft. In this way, they are more certain of the development of their ideas and can create an introduction that is more relevant to their paper as a whole.

Peerediting and Rewriting for Organization

Now you can look at the organization of your essay. Look at the elements of organization that we have studied so far, in particular, the arrangement of the major points of an essay into separate paragraphs and the effectiveness of the introduction.

DIRECTIONS: Exchange papers as you did before. This time, focus on the following organization questions.

1. Mark the principal points and decide if they are logically and clearly organized into separate paragraphs and/or sections of the paper.
2. Read over the introduction again.
   a. What technique is used to introduce the topic?
   b. Is it relevant to the intended reader?
   c. Is it relevant to the topic?
   d. Does it introduce the topic clearly?

    e. Is it interesting?
    f. Make any suggestions needed for improving the introduction.

After carefully considering the evaluation of your peereditor, rewrite your essay based on the changes you have decided to make. Remember to change only what seems right to you.

Proofreading

As you learned in unit 3, it is usually more effective to look for one problem at a time when you proofread.

DIRECTIONS: Proofread this composition several times, searching for a different type of problem each time.

1. Read through one time to find words that sound wrong.
2. Concentrate on sentence boundaries. Decide if each sentence is complete.
    a. Does each clause have a subject and a verb?
    b. Are objects included when necessary?
    c. Does each sentence have at least one independent clause?
3. Locate each verb.
    a. Does it agree in number with its subject?
    b. Is the tense appropriate for the content and meaning of the sentence?
4. Proofread for spelling. Look up the spelling of any words you are unsure of.

Sharing Your Writing

TOPIC A: In a circle, pass the papers on topic A to your left. Read the composition of your classmate. Repeat the process until you have read everyone's composition. Then, in small groups, discuss which compositions are most convincing and which sports or leisure activities you would like to participate in. Did all the groups agree on the most convincing papers? Why or why not?

TOPIC B: If two opposing viewpoints were presented in the papers on the use of science in sports, organize a debate between these two viewpoints. You may wish to work with other class members in a team effort. Each side/team should present its case as clearly as possible to the class and then respond to the points of the opposing side/team. At the end of the debate, the class can vote on the most convincing position.

Keeping a Journal

1. Imagine that you are competing in an event at the Olympic games. What event is it? How does it feel to be a participant in such an event? What are your thoughts and

actions as you wait for your turn to perform? as you give all of your concentration and effort to do your best? as you hear the results of your efforts? Now imagine that you have just come back from a hard day of competition. Write an entry for your personal journal describing that day.

2. Think back to a time when you were under pressure to perform well in some task. Perhaps you were to make an important presentation at school or at work. Perhaps you were involved in an actual sports competition. Read over the questions in the preceding journal topic. Now write an entry about this real-life performance situation and your reactions to it.

UNIT FIVE

CROSSING ECONOMIC BORDERS: BUSINESS AND MANAGEMENT

LESSON 1

'WA' AND THE ART OF AUTO ASSEMBLY

About the Selection:

One important aspect of our society's changes is that modern technology is making our world grow smaller. Cultures that were once distinct and isolated are discovering one another. As time goes on, complex interdependencies are developing between nations. In this next reading selection, we find a perfect example of how different cultures of our world are meeting, perhaps even melding, in the domain of business. Reporter Frank Viviano tells the story of a Japanese and North American business venture at a Northern California automobile factory called Nummi.

Before You Read: Reading with a Purpose

Remember that to be an efficient reader it is important that you determine why you are reading a selection before beginning. In reading this selection, you should try to understand the meaning of the Japanese term *wa*. Why is this concept so great a change from traditional American attitudes in industry? How do you account for the industrialists' feelings of fear and curiosity mentioned in paragraph 1?

'WA' AND THE ART OF AUTO ASSEMBLY
by Frank Viviano

[1]   Across fields burned dry by the California sun, lies the old General Motors automobile plant, teaming anew as United Motor Manufacturing, Inc. or Nummi. Nummi is a corporate venture[1] between General Motors, which once ruled this turf[2] alone, and its most powerful Japanese rival, Toyota. The first such partnership in the United States, it is also something much more novel than that—something that U.S. industrialists have looked forward to with a mixture of fear and curiosity for at least a decade.

[2]   By tacit agreement of GM, Toyota and the United Auto Workers, Nummi is the place where the vaunted[3] Japanese managerial method is to meet its ultimate American test. The experience is so ambitious that it could write the book on industrial procedures for the 21st century.

[3]   Petitioners by the score mass[4] each day in the two-story foyer that serves as the plant's second defense barrier, beyond a high fence and guard post where every car, every visitor, is halted. Contractors, job applicants, ambassadors from the rest of the auto world, often seem disappointed that the scene isn't more visibly Japanese. The industrial rumor mill is so obsessed with Nummi's meaning that visitors half expect to find a sushi bar in the lobby and geishas at the reception desk. "Looks pretty normal to me," a Detroit equipment salesman whispered, as we waited for clearance to enter the inner sanctum.[5]

[4]   But normal it isn't, as I discovered when I was escorted upstairs to meet Nummi executives Kenichi Mizuo and Robert Hendry. For one thing, Hendry, who has 20 years at General Motors behind him, was wearing the same uniform I'd seen on assembly line workers in the parking lot—a gray smock over charcoal pants and a light blue shirt adorned with Nummi's corporate symbol, a small square centered into a larger one. It's a sure bet he never would have been seen dead in a blue collar back at GM headquarters. His job, too, is designed on an alien model, combining public relations, press liaison, government lobbying, assorted financial details and security services, usually separate functions in U.S. auto plants. "Ken" Mizuo, is essentially Hendry's Japanese counterpart, here for the indeterminate[6] period necessary to install the Toyota management concept.

---

[1]**venture:** a speculative undertaking
[2]**turf:** territory
[3]**vaunted:** bragged about
[4]**mass:** gather
[5]**inner sanctum:** private, almost holy area
[6]**indeterminate:** not precisely determined

5 "Concept-wise," Hendry said, "We wanted to start with as much of the Toyota system as possible—to see how much of it we could implement[7] in an American setting. We knew we would have to make modifications—allowances for differences in culture, for example—but the idea was to preserve the basic concept."

6 "We call it *wa*," says Mizuo. "It means cooperation." He smiles broadly. "At Nummi, everybody—union, managers, workers—is working for a common goal. You will find many fewer distinctions here between people, between unskilled and skilled workers, between managers and production employees. There is only one concept at Nummi," he adds. "Team member."

7 Mizuo's assertion might sound glib in the United States, but as the most casual tourist soon appreciates, in Japan it carries the force of religious dogma.[8] To be sure, an executive post there carries greater status than one on the assembly line, but in other ways the Japanese work place is far less rigidly structured than egalitarian America's. "In Japan," said Mizuo, "the custom is not even to specify what job someone is hired for. They are hired to be on the team, and they begin at the bottom, rising until they reach the best possible place for the team, whatever their background. In fact, in the Toyota legal department there are no executives with law degrees, while our accounting department is run by a lawyer with no accounting training." At company headquarters, he added, nearly half the executives were promoted up through the ranks from the factory floor.

8 Although Mizuo and Hendry cleared their throats nervously when asked if America was ready for that kind of revolu-tion, they insisted that Nummi is committed to a radical[9] decentralization of the production process. In place of 84 separate job titles on the conventional U.S. auto plant floor, they explained, Nummi has just three: Each workers is trained to do several different jobs and assigned to a unit of five to seven people—a "team"—under a "team leader." Four such teams comprise[10] a group, which is headed by a group leader.

9 "There are no industrial engineers packing the floor with stopwatches to establish a schedule, no process engineers telling people the right way to do their jobs," said Hendry. "The team members themselves make those decisions. The idea is a pretty dramatic one if you know the history of the automobile industry in America. The concept we're really honing here, the thing that Toyota has pioneered, even in Japan, is replacing the conflict model of labor relations with one based on consensus, on mutual trust and shared responsibility."

10 The feeling that the concept is successful is not limited to management alone. As one group leader and past GM factory worker stated, "We've got good, hard workers in America. Most people want nothing more than to do a good job, their best work. But morale used to be terrible—nobody gave a damn about us or what we had to say. It used to be that if you were a foreman, you were from a different class. But the group leader is right out there on the line sweating with us, asking us our opinion every day, and so are people from the front office. Physically, you'd never even be able to tell who's who, because everyone is wearing the same uniform.

11 "You talk to almost anyone at Nummi

---

[7]**implement:** carry into effect
[8]**dogma:** a system of doctrines or beliefs proclaimed by a church
[9]**radical:** extreme
[10]**comprise:** make up

and you'll hear the same thing: Finally, someone is giving us an opportunity to be treated with respect."

[12]   That was the key. That word: "respect." It has won a vast[11] reservoir of support for Nummi and will most certainly be the determining factor in the successful transfer of Toyota's basic philosophy to American industry. 'Wa' and the Art of Auto Assembly. In America, will it work?

[11]**vast:** very great in area or extent

" 'Wa' and the Art of Auto Assembly" by Frank Viviano, *San Francisco Examiner: Image*, October 6, 1985. Copyright © 1985 Frank Viviano. Adapted and reprinted with permission of the author.

After You Read: Understanding and Using Quotations

This article, based on an interview of two executives at an automobile assembly plant, presents a great deal of its information in the form of statements made by the people interviewed. In some cases, these statements were direct quotes of the interviewee's exact words. In other cases, the author simply reported what had been said without using the speaker's exact words. Learning to recognize and use such **quotations**, both **direct** and **indirect**, is an important skill because it is one way that we can support a point that we are making. Quotations can help to convince the reader that the author's point is valid, especially when the source is an authority on the subject. Let's examine how quotations are used in the passage about Nummi.

DIRECTIONS: Refer to the reading " 'Wa' and the Art of Auto Assembly" to answer the following questions.

1. Paragraphs 5, 6, 9, 10, and 11 consist, primarily, of quotations. Who is the speaker in each paragraph? How do you know?

2. Compare these lines that begin paragraphs 5 and 6.
    "Concept-wise," Hendry said, "we wanted to start with as much of the Toyota system as possible..."
    "We call it 'wa,' " says Mizuo. "It means cooperation."
    The speaker is acknowledged after the quote begins in both cases, but there is a difference in punctuation. Explain why.

3. Find other examples in the reading that have the same punctuation as the examples in question 2.

4. Locate quotations that acknowledge the speaker before the quote.

5. Paragraphs 7 and 8 contain indirect quotes. Locate these statements that are written as reported speech. Rewrite these statements as direct quotations. When we use indirect speech, we *report* on what was said. Notice the changes in pronouns, verb tense, and time words that often occur when we use this form:
    He said, "I can't study any more tonight."
    He said that he couldn't study any more that night.

6. Locate other uses of quotation marks in the reading. Why did the author put these words or phrases in quotes?

7. The quotes in paragraphs 3, 7, 10, and 11 are used to support a previously stated idea. What ideas do they support?

Becoming a Proficient Writer

Generating Ideas

• Freewriting

You have just taken an in-depth look at the article, "'Wa' and the Art of Auto Assembly." First, in a class discussion, and then, in a freewriting, you will expand on some of the ideas that the article exposed you to. In the next exercise, you will use the ideas that you generate in this freewriting.

DIRECTIONS: As a class, come up with a definition of *wa*. Then freewrite on what you think are the advantages and/or the disadvantages of being a worker in a context where *wa* functions. Begin your freewriting with your own definition of *wa*. If you wish, include experiences that you have had that relate to this issue.

• Conducting an Interview

This exercise gives you a chance to conduct an interview and be interviewed. Using the ideas you have just generated in your freewriting, you and a classmate will interview each other about the concepts raised in the article, "'Wa' and the Art of Auto Assembly."

Conducting a successful interview is a challenging task. If you have ever watched a "talk show" on television or listened to an interview on the radio, you may have some ideas about what makes an interview interesting. Before you begin this activity, think back to an interview you have heard or maybe one that you participated in. You might even have the opportunity to listen to one today on radio or television. Try to determine what the interviewer did that made the interview successful. What could the interviewer have done to improve the experience? Did he or she seem prepared? Did the interviewer appear to be listening to the answers of the interviewee? How could you tell? If you watched the interview on television or live, you can address this last question by what you both heard and saw. Remember that body language (gestures, facial expressions, posture, and so on) can play an important role in such an activity. What kinds of nonverbal responses did the interviewer make? Once you have thought about these questions, discuss your ideas about successful interviewing with your partner, in a small group, or with your class.

DIRECTIONS: You and a classmate will interview each other about work and the concept of 'wa' and about cross-cultural work situations.

1. Determine the purpose of the interview.
2. Prepare questions that will help you to achieve your purpose. The following is a

partial list of some of the kinds of questions that you might want to ask. Read through these questions, and then, on a piece of paper, brainstorm other questions that you might want to ask.

a. Briefly describe a job you do, used to do, or plan to do and its context. (A company would be the ideal context.)

b. Does the concept of 'wa' function in this particular work situation? How?

c. Describe the workers' morale, how they feel about their jobs and the work situation. What aspects of the job make the morale high or low?

d. What could be done to improve the morale? Could 'wa' improve the situation?

e. What would you tell someone about your culture that would help them to better understand your work situation?

f. Do you believe that corporations in which two or more cultures work together are a good idea? Why or why not?

g. Would you like to work in such a corporation? Explain.

3. Conduct the interview, taking careful notes so that you can write about it and report on it later.

4. Switch roles so that you each have an opportunity to be the interviewer and the interviewee.

● Roleplaying

Now that you have played the roles of both interviewer and interviewee, you can share the information that you have learned with several other classmates. To make this task very directed, your group will pretend to be a commission chosen by a specific country to decide whether or not to permit a company from another culture to join with a company from your culture. Each member of the commission was to prepare for this decision-making meeting by interviewing a worker about the issue (the interview you just conducted). Now your job is to report your findings so that the decision can be supported by real-life examples.

DIRECTIONS: Work with one or two other teams to follow these steps.

1. Each interview team joins one or two other teams.

2. Each group of four or six chooses a secretary to take notes and a chairperson to head the meeting.

3. The chairperson then conducts a meeting in which all group members take turns reporting on the interviews.

4. The groups discuss the issue of multinational corporations, finding specific examples to support their ideas.

5. Each group decides on its recommendation.

6. Each group reports its decision to the class, explaining the idea that helped the group reach that decision.

LESSON 2

LEARNING FROM FOREIGN MANAGEMENT

About the Selection:

As the reading in lesson 1 suggests, an important change occurring in the worldwide business community is that it is opening up to cross-cultural business arrangements. In this next reading, "Learning from Foreign Management," Peter Drucker, a celebrated author who is considered by some to be the master teacher of modern management, explores this same issue in an article published in the *Wall Street Journal*, a leading business newspaper in the United States.

The First Reading

Before You Read: Skimming for the Main Idea

As we have mentioned earlier in this text, we can often increase our understanding of a piece of writing by becoming familiar with it before we actually read it fully. The following reading lends itself very well to one reading strategy called **skimming**. To **skim** we read quickly to obtain the general idea of a passage. In this next reading, look for the general topic in the first paragraph, and then read the first sentence of every paragraph to determine how the author separates his main points.

The main idea of the article is_____

_____

_____

As You Read: Looking for the Main Idea

Now read the article to see if its main idea corresponds to the answer you gave in the preceding exercise.

LEARNING FROM FOREIGN MANAGEMENT
by Peter F. Drucker

1   "What can we learn from American management?" was the question asked all over the world only 10 years ago. Now it is perhaps time to ask: What can American management learn from others in the free world, and especially from management in Western Europe and Japan? For Europe and Japan now have the managerial edge[1] in many of the areas which we used to consider American strengths, if not American monopolies.[2]

2   First, foreign managers increasingly demand responsibility from their employees, all the way down to the lowliest blue-collar worker on the factory floor. They are putting to work the tremendous improvement in the education and skill of the labor force that has been accomplished in this century. The Japanese are famous for their "quality circles" and their "continuous learning." Employees at all levels come together regularly, sometimes once a week, more often twice a month, to address the question: "What can we do to improve what we already are doing?" In Germany, a highly skilled senior worker known as the "Meister" acts as teacher, assistant and standard-setter, rather than as "supervisor" and "boss."

3   Second, foreign managers have thought through their benefits policies more carefully. "Fringes" in the United States are now as wide as in any other country, that is they amount to some 40 cents for

[1]**edge:** advantage
[2]**monopolies:** commodities controlled exclusively

each dollar paid in cash wages. But in this country, many benefits fail to help the individual employee. In many families, for instance, both husband and wife are docked the full family health insurance premium at work, even though one insurance policy would be sufficient. And we pay full Social Security charges for the married working woman, even though married working women under our Social Security system may never see a penny of their money paid back into their accounts.

Benefits According to Need

[4]   By contrast, foreign managements, especially those of Japan and Germany, structure benefits according to the needs of recipients.[3] The Japanese, for instance, set aside dowry money for young unmarried women, while they provide housing allowances to men in their early thirties with young families. In England, a married woman in the labor force can opt out of a large part of old-age insurance if her husband already pays for the couple at his place of employment.

[5]   Third, foreign managers take marketing seriously. In most American companies marketing still means no more than systematic selling. Foreigners today have absorbed more fully the true meaning of marketing: knowing what is value for the customer.

[6]   American managers can learn from the way foreigners look at their products, technology and strategies from the point of view of the market rather than vice versa. Foreigners are increasingly thinking in terms of market structure, trying to define specific market niches[4] for their products,

and designing their business with a marketing strategy in mind. The Japanese automobile companies are but one example. Few companies are so attentive to the market as the high-technology and high-fashion entrepreneurs of northern Italy.

[7]   It is not correct, as is so often asserted in this country, that Japanese and Western European businesses subordinate profits. Indeed the return on total assets is conspicuously[5] higher today in a great many foreign businesses than it is in this country, especially if profits are adjusted for inflation. But the foreign manager has increasingly learned to say, "It is my job to earn a proper profit on what the market wants to buy." We still, by and large, try to say in this country, "What is our product with the highest profit margin? Let's try to sell that, and sell it hard."

[8]   Incidentally, when the foreign manager says "market," he tends to think of the world economy. Very few Japanese companies actually depend heavily on exports. And yet it is the rare Japanese business which does not start out with the world economy in marketing, even if its own sales are predominantly in the Japanese home market.

[9]   Fifth, foreign managements keep separate and discrete[6] those areas where short-term results are the proper measurements and those where results should be measured over longer time spans, such as innovation, product development, product introduction and manager development. The quarterly P and L is taken as seriously in Tokyo and Osaka as it is in New York and Chicago; and, with the strong role that the banks plays in the management of German companies, the quarterly P and L[7] is probably taken more seriously in Frankfurt than

---

[3]**recipients:** ones that receive
[4]**niches:** suitable positions
[5]**conspicuously:** noticably
[6]**discrete:** consisting of distinct parts
[7]**P and L:** profit and loss

it is in the U.S. But outside the U.S., the quarterly P and L is increasingly being confined to the 90% or so of the budget that is concerned with operations and with the short term.

[11]   There is then a second budget, usually no more than a few percent of the total, which deals with those areas in which expenditures have to be maintained over a long period of time to get any results. By separating short term operating budgets from longer term investment or opportunities budgets, foreign companies can plan for the long haul. They can control expenditures over the long term and get results for long term efforts and investments.

[12]   Sixth, managers in large Japanese, German and French companies see themselves as national assets and leaders responsible for the development of proper policies in the national interest. One good example may be a group that came to see me six months ago. The chief executive officers of the 40 largest Japanese companies came to discuss how Japan should adjust to demographic changes; official retirement age is still 55 in Japan, while life expectancy is now closer to 80.

[13]   "We don't want to discuss with you," said the leader of the group, "what we in Japanese business should be doing. Our agenda is what Japan should be doing and what the best policies are in the national interest. Only after we have thought through the right national policies, and have defined and publicized them, are we going to think about the implications for business and for our companies. Indeed we should postpone[8] discussing economics altogether until we have understood what the right social policies are and what is best for the individual Japanese and for the country altogether. Who else besides the heads of Japan's large companies can really look at such a problem from all aspects? To whom else can the country really look for guidance and leadership in such a tremendous change as that of the age structure of our population?"

[14]   Any American executive, at all conversant with our management literature, will now say: "What else is new? Every one of these things I have known for 30 years or so." But this is precisely the point. What we can learn from foreign management is not what to do. What we can learn is to do it.

[8]**postpone:** delay

Peter F. Drucker, "Learning from Foreign Management," *Wall Street Journal.* Reprinted by permission of *Wall Street Journal*/Dow Jones & Company, Inc.

After You Read: Understanding Specialized Vocabulary

When we are exposed to a new situation, we often encounter new terms that are specific to that situation. Learning these terms is like unlocking a door that opens to an unexplored world. They are the key that permits us to further our understanding of a particular field. In the passage "Learning from Foreign Management," we encounter many such terms. To help you to unlock the door to the world of business, we have isolated a variety of nouns that are specific to the field of business. These nouns fall into two categories: nouns relating to money matters, and those relating to business management practices.

DIRECTIONS: First, locate the following terms in the reading. Use the techniques you have learned for understanding vocabulary from context to guess their meanings. Then fit the appropriate words into the following paragraphs.

wages   expenditure   assets
investments   inflation   budget
profit margin

When a company needs to calculate its yearly _____ to determine

how it should manage its money for the following year, it must take many financial

aspects into account. It must consider what it costs to have the business operate. One

such _____ would be the _____ that are paid to its em-

ployees. Another area the company must examine is what its total _____

are, in other words, what the true value of the business is. In calculating this, the

company must take into account any _____ that it has made, in the stock

market, for example, and what their market value is. Being careful to consider unknown

factors, such as what the possible rate of _____ might be for the following

year, the accountants can then determine the possible _____ that the

company can expect to make on its products.

strategies   entrepreneurs   operations
policies   chief executive officer   agenda

Today's wise _____ must be thoughtful managers on many levels. If

they are serving as the _____ of their company, they must make careful

decisions concerning overall company _____ that will have a direct effect

on the success of the business endeavor. It is essential that they employ _____

that are known to increase productivity. They should, for example, have a daily

_____ to ensure the smooth functioning of the various business _____.

The Second Reading

As You Read: Recognizing the Author's Plan

In the first reading you discovered that the author of "Learning from Foreign Management" stated his topic in the first paragraph and then separated his main points into six categories over fourteen paragraphs. In this second reading you will determine what each paragraph is about.

DIRECTIONS: Working with a classmate, restate the topic of each paragraph, using your own words as much as possible. To help you get started, we have provided you with the topics of a few paragraphs.

Paragraph 1 _____

_____

Paragraph 2 Foreign managers ask all workers, regardless of their rank, to take responsibility.

Paragraph 3 _____

_____

Paragraph 4 Foreign managers offer benefits that correspond to the particular employee's needs.

Paragraph 5 _____

_____

Paragraph 6 Foreign managers are considering more and more the market and are making managerial decisions based on their findings.

Paragraph 7 _____

_____

Paragraph 8 Foreign managers consider the world economy in marketing even if they don't do very much exporting.

Paragraph 9 _____

_____

Paragraph 10 _____

_____

Paragraph 11 _____

_____

Paragraph 12 _____

_____

Paragraph 13 _____

_____

Paragraph 14 _____

_____

After You Read

• Understanding Organization: Using a Flowchart and Recognizing the Thesis Statement

With the information you have just provided on the main idea of each paragraph, you can now begin to discover the relationship of one paragraph to the next. One way to do this is to fit such information into a **flowchart**. A flowchart, as we use it in this text, is a diagram that shows the logical relationship of ideas in a piece of writing. You can think of it as the skeleton of a passage, the underlying structure that maintains the posture or shape of a piece of writing.

A flowchart establishes the connection between the smaller segments that make up a complete passage. *It begins with the most general ideas of the piece and works down to the most specific.* The lowest items on a flowchart are the most specific aspects of the piece of writing; the highest are the most general. For example, the first paragraph in the Drucker article states that North American management has a lot to learn from foreign management. This is a more general concept than the subject of the second paragraph, which discusses one of the six techniques that American managers could learn. The remaining five techniques are divided over the next eleven paragraphs; this means that the purpose of some paragraphs is to give more specific information about some of the five techniques.

DIRECTIONS: Following is a flowchart that has been partially completed. With a classmate, complete the chart by referring to the answers you wrote in the preceding exercise. You need not rewrite the information; instead, use only the number of the paragraph to identify it.

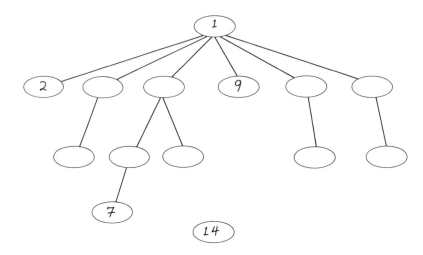

As you can see by the preceding flowchart, all of the paragraphs in the article relate back, either directly or indirectly, to the first paragraph. In English writing, we often find this same pattern. As we discussed in unit 4, the first paragraph (in some cases, the first few paragraphs, as in *Ultra Sports* in unit 4) serves as an introduction to the topic and prepares the reader for what is to come in the rest of the passage. Looking more closely, we will see that the last two sentences of paragraph 1 present the reader with a clear idea of what to expect from the rest of the passage. We call this a **thesis statement**. This thesis statement is a kind of "contract" between the writer and the reader. The writer makes a promise to the reader, and the reader expects that promise to be kept. Consider what Peter Drucker's contract promised to you, the reader. Did he keep his promise?

● Understanding Organization: Recognizing the Topic Sentence

As you can see from the preceding exercise, the paragraphs in the article by Peter Drucker relate to each other very logically. One idea leads to the next in an ordered pattern. We can find this pattern in individual paragraphs as well, particularly in all **body paragraphs** (everything other than the introduction and the conclusion). Let's examine the organization of a body paragraph in the Drucker article.

DIRECTIONS: Fit the sentences in paragraph 2 of the Peter Drucker article into the flowchart on the next page.

Once again, the logical pattern between ideas is obvious. Just as the thesis statement serves as a contract to the reader, preparing the reader for what is to come in the passage, the first sentence of some paragraphs functions in the same way. We call this sentence a **topic sentence**. In academic writing we often, but not always, have topic sentences, and they are *usually* the first sentence of the paragraph. Once we have read the topic sentence, we should be able to guess what the rest of the paragraph is about. Try to test this out by reading only the first sentence in paragraph 9. Write down what you expect the rest of the paragraph to be about. Now, read the rest of the paragraph to see if

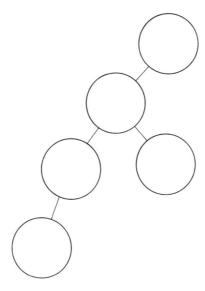

the topic sentence was a reliable "contract." Remember that while we frequently encounter paragraphs that begin with a topic sentence, not all paragraphs follow this pattern. Some paragraphs contain a topic sentence at the end, some in the middle, and some have none at all.

Becoming a Proficient Writer

Guided Writing: Using Deductive Organization

The paragraph organization that you have just been working with is based on **deductive** thinking. You are given a statement that is then supported by more specific statements. This is one important way that paragraphs can be organized. The following exercise asks you to apply this concept.

DIRECTIONS: Using the concept of deductive paragraph organization, arrange the following sentences in appropriate order. If you wish, you can use a flowchart to help you with this exercise. You might even choose to recopy the sentences onto slips of paper so that you can rearrange them as if they were a puzzle.

1. In one generation, many of these families have faced an adjustment from remote rural lifestyles to urban communities.
2. In Sao Paolo, many workers are drawn from very poor *favelas* of the city, while in Piracicaba most of the work force were formerly cane cutters on the surrounding sugar plantations.
3. Companies like Castle and Cooke, which grows pineapples on a mountainside plantation on an island in the Philippines, or Caterpillar Tractor, which manufac-

tures construction and agricultural equipment in Sao Paolo and nearby Piracicaba in Brazil, introduce new products in these countries and new ways of making them.

4. In Third World countries, multinational corporations become an agent of development, a foreign agent of change.

5. They contribute to economic development and, in the process, change people's lives.

6. Castle and Cooke has drawn 9,000 workers to its pineapple raising and canning operation, with many families migrating from areas more than 300 miles away.

7. Caterpillar employs about 2,800 workers in its Brazilian operations.

You can see how each sentence has a *purpose*, whether it be to present the main idea, offer supporting points, or give further evidence to develop a specific point. Depending on this purpose, each sentence will also have a position.

LESSON 3

COMPOSING
ON YOUR OWN

This unit's composing task will ask you to incorporate much of what you have learned so far. Since you have several drafts in which to accomplish this task, remember that you can address different aspects of the writing process at different stages. As you proceed, maintain your focus on the particular element that each draft addresses.

The First Draft

Choosing a Topic

DIRECTIONS: Choose one of the following topics to write about in an essay of at least 500 words.

A. Using a business you are familiar with, answer the question, "What are the old things that should be abandoned?" and tell why. Then mention what innovation, new products, or new markets you would invest in with the newly available resources. If you wish, you could write about the school you are attending by considering it a business that earns money through tuition and/or other means and that spends money on teachers' salaries, supplies, maintenance, and the like.

B. Discuss how the Japanese concept of *wa* relates to your present job, a past job, or a job you plan to have in the future. Only if you have never worked should you choose the last possibility. As you have no doubt discovered, it is much easier to write about something that you have had experience with.

C.   Discuss the differences in benefits policies between two countries or two jobs that you are familiar with. Then describe a benefits policy that you believe would be ideal.

Generating Ideas

Now use one or more of the techniques you have learned to generate ideas as well as any of the related ideas that you produced in the various activities of this unit. Take this step of the process as seriously as the final steps. It creates the foundation for your paper. Exploring your ideas in a free and flowing way lays the groundwork for an interesting paper and may even allow you to discover ideas as you write.

Writing the First Draft

At this stage you need to decide to whom you are addressing this essay and your purpose for writing it. You should also have some ideas as to what the major points are that will prove your idea. These essential concerns will establish a plan for your essay.

DIRECTIONS: Complete the following sentences:

1.   I am writing about this topic because _____

_____

_____.

2.   The main point I want to make is _____

_____

_____.

3.   I plan to show my reader that this is true by writing about the following ideas:

      a.   _____

      b.   _____

      c.   _____

4. The audience I am addressing is _____

_____.

Now write the first draft, keeping these decisions in mind. Also remember to include showing details that will help to support your ideas.

Peerediting and Revising

DIRECTIONS: Trade papers with a classmate. Complete the following statements.

1. The writer's main point is _____

_____

_____.

2. The writer proves that this is true by writing about the following ideas:

    a. _____

    b. _____

    c. _____

3. The intended audience appears to be _____

_____.

4. The writer's purpose seems to be _____

_____

_____.

5. The writer uses specific showing details, such as _____

_____

_____.

(Mark places on the draft where showing should be added.)

6. The aspects of this paper that help to achieve the purpose are _____

_____

_____.

The writer might have done the following to better achieve the purpose: _____

_____

_____

Once you have finished peerediting, carefully compare your answers with the writer's self-evaluation of his or her plan. This should tell if each writer actually accomplished what he or she had planned. Then discuss with your partner what improvements you could each make in this first draft. After you have decided what you want to change in your essay, make the appropriate revisions. Remember that at the first draft stage, you are focusing on how adequate the writer's ideas are to communicate the message successfully.

The Second Draft

Writing the Second Draft

For this draft, we want you to apply the concepts of thesis statement and topic sentences that you have learned about in this unit. Just as Peter Drucker announces the subject of his article at the end of the first paragraph (the introduction), so could you introduce your topic in the first paragraph. Make sure that your introduction also catches the reader's attention, as we discussed in unit 4. Your next paragraphs could contain topic sentences that prepare the reader for what the paragraph is about.

DIRECTIONS: Exchange papers with a classmate. Fill out the following questionnaire that asks you to analyze your partner's paper. Keep in mind what you learned about your strengths and weaknesses as an editor in the peerediting experience in unit 2 when you compared your perceptions with your teacher's.

1. Before reading the entire paper, read the first paragraph. Underline the thesis statements. What do you expect the paper to be about?

_____

_____

_____

2. Now, locate the sentence(s) of each body paragraph that contains the main idea. Write what each paragraph is about.

_____

_____

_____

_____

_____

3. Read the entire essay. Write the main point of the essay here.

_____

_____

_____

_____

4. Compare your answers to item 1 and item 3. Are they the same? If not, write another thesis statement that would better inform the reader of the main point.

_____

_____

_____

5. Draw a flowchart to show the paragraph organization of the essay.

6. Review the answers to the preceding questions with your partner. Each of you should take notes on areas you need to improve in your own essay.

7. Tell your classmate what you liked most about the essay.

Go over the peerediting guidelines one by one, referring to the notes you took during the peerediting session. Determine the areas you should improve on, and delete, change, or add anything you wish on your draft. Remember that your paper might look rather messy, but this is expected. Relax and enjoy this step of the process where you need not worry about neatness or even legibility. Once you have completed this process, rewrite your paper. Finally, go back over your notes and the guidelines to make sure that you have made all of the changes necessary.

Peerediting in a Group

Now, with your peerediting partner, join another peerediting team to make a group of four. Pass your papers to one another so that everyone can read all of the papers. For every paper you read, note what you like most about the paper and what areas the student could improve on. Make sure that your comments are limited to the content and organization and not to the grammar or mechanics. Share the ideas you have about each other's papers. Your original partner should end the discussion about your paper by making a statement as to how this draft was an improvement on the last draft.

Revising

It is likely that after the group editing session you will want to revise your paper. If your revisions are not major, you could proofread at this point.

Proofreading

Each time we have asked you to proofread in previous units, we have given you direction as to what to look for in the proofreading and how to go about it. We are exposing you to various methods of proofreading; our goal is to help you to establish your own method that is best suited to your needs. You may want to use any one or a combination of these methods depending on the kinds of mistakes you are making and your level of proficiency in English.

In any case, proofreading should have several steps. One step you have already begun using involves learning to rely on what sounds right. Knowing when something sounds right without relying on grammar rules is called **intuition**. You already have maximum intuition in your native language, and you are establishing intuition in English. Now you can learn to use your English intuition to help you to proofread. There are several ways to go about this. One way is to read your paper aloud to yourself to listen to the sound of your words. Perhaps you could have a friend or classmate read your paper to you. Or you can even tape record your paper and listen to the sound of your words as you play it back. This technique will become more and more useful as your English proficiency increases.

Once you have listened for what sounds right, you can then go through your paper looking for one grammatical consideration at a time. You should have an idea now as to the kinds of grammatical problems you have, so choose three of your specific grammatical problems and focus on them.

Sharing Your Writing

You have already looked at the papers of several other classmates. Now you will share what you have written with the rest of your class. Sit in a circle with the other students in your class. Pass your paper to the right. Read the paper that has been passed to you and take notes on anything in the paper that you liked or were interested in. When you have finished reading, pass that paper to your right and continue the process until your own paper is returned to you. Your class will discuss all of the strong points that were discovered in these papers.

Keeping a Journal

1. The reading in lesson 1 of this unit raised the issue of respect given to employees at their jobs. Whether you are working or studying, this is certainly an issue that you must have encountered. Think back to a moment that stands out in your mind when you were treated with either respect or disrespect, or some time when you treated someone else with respect or disrespect. Describe that moment and discuss your feelings about this issue as they relate to the experience you have chosen to write about.

2. The world of business and finance has had far-reaching effects in our modern times. We are surrounded by evidence of the great influence this aspect of life has had on our surroundings. Think of a change that you know of or that you have experienced personally that is due to financial or business interests. Describe this change and give your opinion as to whether or not this change is positive.

UNIT SIX

PARENTS, CHILDREN, AND THE FAMILY UNIT: ANTHROPOLOGY

LESSON 1

THE ARAPESH

About the Selection:

In this next passage, "The Arapesh," Melvin Tumin introduces us to the evidence that the world-renowned anthropologist, Margaret Mead, gathered on the Arapesh, a tribal society from Papua, New Guinea. At the time of the study, in 1930, the roles of men and women in the Arapesh society were quite different from the traditional, sex-related roles of most modern societies. The observations of anthropologist Mead raise some interesting questions about the basic nature of men and women.

Before You Read: Exploring Your Own Ideas

An interesting activity that can help you to respond fully to an article is first to establish your own ideas about the topic. Before reading, complete the following questions in regard to your own society. You will have a chance to share your ideas after reading the article.

Men and women in my society live in a spirit of (cooperation? competition?)

_____

Men and women in my society share responsibility in

_____

People in my society believe that men and women are

_____

As You Read: Reading with a Purpose

Compare your views expressed in the sentence completion exercise with the attitudes of the Arapesh regarding the identity and roles of men and women.

THE ARAPESH
by Melvin M. Tumin

Arapesh life is organized around the way that women and men, physically different and possessing different abilities, meet in a common[1] adventure. This adventure is primarily maternal, loving, and directed away from the self toward the needs of the next generation. In the Arapesh culture, women and men do different things for the

[1]**common:** shared

same reasons. It is a culture in which men are not expected to have one set of motives and women another. If men are given more authority, it is because authority is a necessary evil that someone, the freer partner, must carry.

WHO DOES WHAT. When the Arapesh are questioned about the division of labor, they answer: cooking everyday food, bringing firewood and water, weeding and carrying—these are women's work. Cooking ceremonial food, carrying pigs and heavy logs, housebuilding, sewing the material for the roofs of the huts, clearing and building fences, carving, hunting, and growing sweet potatoes—these are men's work. Making ornaments and the care of the children—these are the work of both men and women. If the wife's task is more important at the moment than the husband's—if there are no greens for the evening meal, or a leg of meat must be carried to neighbors in the next village—the husband stays at home and takes care of the baby.

ARAPESH ATTITUDES TOWARD CHILDREN. The Arapesh regard both women and men as naturally gentle, sensitive, and cooperative. Adults of both sexes are willing and able to consider their own needs as less important than the needs of those who are younger and weaker—and to receive satisfaction from doing so. They are delighted with the part of parenthood that we consider to be especially maternal—loving care for the little child and the selfless delight in that child's progress toward maturity. The parent takes no self-centered pleasure in this progress. He or she makes no extreme demands for great devotion in this world, or for ancestor worship in the next. To the Arapesh, the child is not a way to guarantee that the individual's identity will be carried on. The parents do not use children as a way to keep some small and grasping hold on eternal life.

In some societies, the child is merely a possession, perhaps the most valuable of all—more valuable than houses and lands, pigs and dogs. Yet, in these societies, the child is still a possession to be boasted of to others. But such a picture is meaningless to the Arapesh. Their sense of possession, even of the simplest material object, is just about nonexistent. Far more important to them is a sense of the needs and duties of others.

LIFE GOALS. To the Arapesh, the world is a garden that must be cultivated. But it must not be cultivated for themselves, not in pride and boasting, not for hoarding[2] and then lending out while charging a high interest. Rather, the purpose is that the sweet potatoes and the dogs and the pigs and, most of all, the children may grow. From this whole attitude flow many of the Arapesh traits—the lack of conflict between old and young, the lack of jealousy or envy, and the emphasis on cooperation. Cooperation is easy when everyone is wholeheartedly committed to a common project from which not just one of the participants will benefit. The Arapesh regard men in the same way we regard women— as the gentle and careful parent.

[2]**hoarding:** accumulating a supply

Adapted version of "The Arapesh" from *Foundations in Social Studies: Male and Female in Today's World* by Melvin M. Tumin, copyright © 1980 by Harcourt Brace Jovanovich, Inc., reprinted by permission of the publisher. "The Arapesh" is an adaptation originally based on material from *Sex and Temperament in Three Primitive Societies* by Margaret Mead, copyright 1935, 1950, 1963 by Margaret Mead, reprinted by permission of William Morrow & Co., Inc.

After You Read

● Discovering the Main Idea

You have just read a passage that draws conclusions about the society, the Arapesh. One of the greatest values of learning about the attitudes and values of another culture is that it gives you perspective on your own culture. By seeing the similarities and differences between your culture and the cultures of other societies, you can better understand your own society and its values.

DIRECTIONS: Complete the following sentences about the Arapesh.

The Arapesh live in the spirit of _____ .

They share responsibility in _____ .

They believe that men and women are _____

_____ .

Compare your answers to this sentence completion exercise with your classmates' answers. You may refer to the text if you wish. Discuss the details in the article that support your answers. Then, in small groups, compare these answers about the Arapesh with the conclusions you and your fellow classmates have drawn about your own societies. Think of examples to support these statements about your own society. In other words, try to remember, in your past experiences, what you have observed, experienced, or learned about that caused you to have this opinion.

● Using Supporting Evidence

You will notice that this activity asks you to think of examples which have influenced you to develop your opinion about your society's attitudes. This aspect of the assignment underlines the importance of **supporting evidence.** We each have had specific experiences in our lives, or we have learned about the experiences of others. These exposures have molded the opinions we hold. When we communicate these opinions (in speaking or in writing), we need to share these details with our audience to better convince them that our point of view is valid. These details can come from a number of sources, and these sources must always be reliable. They can be **examples** or **personal experiences** of our own or of someone we have heard or read about. They might be **facts** or **statistics.** They might take the form of **physical descriptions.** Whatever form these details take, they must be *relevant*, convincing, *reliable*, and *specific* (remember our discussions of showing in unit 2). Later in this lesson you will practice using supporting evidence.

● Recognizing Cohesive Devices

One very important element of written language that helps readers to better understand what they are reading is the use of **cohesive devices.** Cohesive devices are words and phrases that the writer weaves into the passage to increase the reader's comprehension. These devices encourage the reader to refer back to previous statements in the passage. By having to recall previously stated information, the reader understands the passage as a whole, as a group of ideas that are logically related. Often this "back reference" occurs so quickly that the reader is not even aware of it. In fact, most writers use at least some cohesive devices automatically. These devices occur in various forms. They may be:

reference pronouns (*he, she, his, hers,* etc.)

demonstrative pronouns (*those, this,* etc.)

demonstrative adjectives (*this* book, *those* books, etc.)

repetition of key words or phrases

synonyms

articles

transitional words or phrases (see unit 3, lesson 2).

Paragraph 3 of "The Arapesh" contains various types of cohesive devices. Let's examine how the devices employed in paragraph 3 increase our understanding of the paragraph.

DIRECTIONS: For each underlined word or phrase in the following passage, find the previously stated information that the word or phrase refers to. Circle that information and draw an arrow to it from the underlined word or phrase that refers to it.

The Arapesh regard both women and men as naturally gentle, sensitive, and cooperative. Adults of both sexes are willing and able to consider their own needs as less important then the needs of those who are younger and weaker— and to receive satisfaction from doing so. They are delighted with the part of parenthood that we consider to be especially maternal—loving care for the little child and the selfless delight in that child's progress toward maturity. The parent takes no self-centered pleasure in this progress. He or she makes no extreme demands for great devotion in this world, or for ancestor worship in the next. To the Arapesh, the child is not a way to guarantee that the individual's identity will be carried on. The parents do not use children as a way to keep some small and grasping hold on eternal life.

Becoming a Proficient Writer

Generating Ideas: Freewriting

You have looked at the evidence gathered by Margaret Mead on the Arapesh society. This evidence gives us an understanding of the way that sexual differences among the Arapesh affect the *roles* (what people should do and what their responsibilities and rights are) and the *identities* (what men and women are like) of the Arapesh men and women. Attitudes about the roles and the identities of men and women exist in every society and have been, throughout the years, an important topic of discussion. On the next page, are quotations about the roles and identities of men and women which come from several different cultures. As you read them the first time, try to notice your immediate reaction to each quote.

"Women are so much more honest than men. A woman says: 'I am jealous.' A man covers it up with a system of philosophy, a book of literary criticism, a study of psychology."

-ANAIS NIN

French-American writer (1933)

"Women, in general, want to be loved for what they are and men for what they accomplish. The first for their looks and charm, the latter for their actions."

-THEODOR REIK
Austrian psychologist (early 1900's)

"The whole of education of women ought to be relative to men. To please them. To be useful to them. To make themselves loved and honored by them. To educate them when young. To care for them when grown. To counsel them. And to make life sweet and agreeable to them. These are the duties of women at all times and what should be taught them from their infancy."

-JEAN JACQUES ROUSSEAU
French philosopher and writer (mid 1700's)

"A husband is a woman's first ornament, though he himself dress plainly. When she has no husband she is not adorned [beautified], no matter what ornament she wears."

-ANCIENT HINDU PROVERB

"Man's love is of man's life a thing apart 'Tis woman's whole existence."

-LORD BYRON

English poet (early 1800"s)

"Woman is the creator and fosterer of life. Man has been the mechanizer and destroyer of life."

-ASHLEY MONTAGU
British anthropologist (mid 1900's)

Illustrations from *Foundations in Social Studies: Male and Female in Today's World* by Melvin M. Tumin, copyright © 1980 by Harcourt Brace Javanovich, Inc., reprinted by permission of the publisher.

DIRECTIONS: After reading the quotations, choose three that interested you the most, and freewrite on each one. You can choose quotes that you either agree with or disagree with, but try to choose the ones that you have the strongest reaction to.

Sharing Ideas: Debating

Now that you have recorded your reactions to some of the quotes in the previous exercise, you can use these reactions as the basis of a debate on one of the quotations. This activity will require that you organize your ideas and that you use relevant and specific evidence to support your opinion.

DIRECTIONS: After determining with your class which quotes created the greatest interest, form small groups made up of students who had similar reactions to the same quote. Hopefully there will be groups with opposing opinions. If not, your group might be asked to argue for the opposite view. Each group will then prepare for a debate by following these steps.

1. Find ideas to support your reaction.
   a. Brainstorm.
   b. Review the brainstormed ideas to determine which ones are the most valid, the most worthwhile.
   c. Organize the ideas by combining ones that are related and then putting them in an order that would make for the most convincing argument.
   d. Think of supporting evidence to defend each idea. To determine if your evidence is convincing, imagine that you are a member of the opposing group. Does the evidence help to sway (begin to change) your opinion? (In other words, is it relevant and believable?) Is it sufficient to actually change your opinion or, at least, convince you that the individual point is valid?
2. Find ideas that you think the opposing group will use to argue their point.
   a. Brainstorm.
   b. Find ideas that you think the opposing group will use to argue their point.
   c. Fit these additions into the organization of your presentation.
3. Determine who will present each section of your presentation. Be sure to plan an introduction and a conclusion.

Now it's time to meet the opposing group in a debate.

1. Each group presents its arguments, beginning with the affirmative side.
2. The second group then may ask the first group questions about their position.
3. The first group answers the questions and then asks questions of group 2.
4. Group 2 answers the questions.
5. The class votes to decide which group had the most convincing argument. (Be sure to base this evaluation on the relevance and strength of the ideas and the evidence used to support the ideas.)

LESSON 2

THE NUCLEAR FAMILY: WOMEN'S WORK IN THE HOME

About the Selection:

In lesson 1 you read about a society whose roles for men and women were different than the roles expected of men and women in many other societies. The next selection examines certain traditional roles of adults in societies where the nuclear family (mother, father, and children, living in one household) has been considered the norm. This selection, "The Nuclear Family: Women's Work in the Home," by Joan Kelly, is taken from a textbook entitled, *Household and Kin.* It examines and questions the tasks performed by many twentieth-century women and leads you to see how this, like so many other aspects of our modern world, is changing.

The First Reading

Before You Read: Exploring Your Own Ideas

Through the activities in lesson 1 you might have changed your views or reaffirmed the beliefs you already held about the roles and identities of men and women. Taking your response to lesson 1 into consideration, complete the following sentence with a brief statement of your personal view on the roles of both sexes in your society.

A man's/woman's job should be

_____

_____

_____.

As You Read: Discovering the Main Idea

Compare your preceding statement with what the author of the selection appears to think the job of men or women should be.

THE NUCLEAR FAMILY: Women's Work in the Home
By Joan Kelly

[1] For most of us, the family meets many of our needs for love and support. We tend to think that all families are almost as varied as people. Families differ from society to society, and they have changed over time. Today's nuclear family is a good example of a changing family, one that has evolved into its present state and is still changing. This type of family descends from the preindustrial household/family. Industrialization was the main reason for the change in the family pattern of the household. With industrialization, goods and services came to be produced outside the household. The household ceased to be a center of production—although it remained as an economic and residential unit for its members. Because this phenomenon obliged the men to work outside of the home, the women became isolated in a new role inside of the home, a role that was to have a long-lasting effect. Until as late as the 1970s, the majority of married women in the industrialized United States worked exclusively in their own homes. Because the father's responsibilities took him outside of the home, most twentieth-century mothers were left to spend their days doing housework and caring for the children, regardless of their interests, capabilities, or individual natures.

[2] Housework is a catchall term that covers a number of tasks done at home. Obtaining food is one aspect of housework. For some families, food raising is still a part of household work. Historically, the more men did socially organized wage work, the

more women and children became responsible for the farming, gardening, raising of chickens, and so forth that supplied some of the family's food. This happens when the family still owns or rents some land. As urban life grew at the expense of rural life, however, food was bought rather than raised. Then shopping became a basic part of housekeeping.

3   Cleaning, preparing, cooking, and serving food in the form of meals call for different skills. Contemporary housewives report that next to child rearing, they like cooking most among their various tasks. It is creative and is usually appreciated. Cleaning up after meals, cleaning the home so that it is orderly and usable, keeping the furnishings and clothing of the family in good condition (and in an earlier time, making cloth and clothing), make up yet another complex of jobs. As skills, laundering, ironing, and mending bear[1] little relation to each other, or to housecleaning, and many housewives say they are not particularly satisfying tasks. They are monotonous because they are constantly repeated and never completed. And they are generally not appreciated. This work is noticed only when it is *not* done—when a shirt is missing a button, a bed not made, a floor not clean.

4   Add child care to housework, and we begin to see why the job of "housewife," according to a study done in the 1970s, takes an average of seventy-seven hours a week. Most housewives who have been surveyed say that child rearing[2] is the most rewarding part of their work. They also speak of the conflicts it sets up with the other demands of housework and of life in general. The care of children has little in common with housekeeping—except that in nuclear family arrangements, both are carried out in the private home, usually by the same person: the mother. Child care requires a set of skills and interests that are sometimes directly opposed to those required by housekeeping—and by husband care. Should one keep the floors clean or let the children play? Does one follow the rhythms of young life or force children into the schedule of a working father?

5   Moreover, not every woman has the attitudes and interests child care calls for, or can sustain[3] an interest in children all day long, day after day. Infants need and have a right to close attention, feeding, fondling, changing, and stimulation for play and learning. Young children also need and deserve loving attention to their bodily, emotional, and imaginative needs. Some mothers are fully satisfied with their daily work in the home. Others have conflicting feelings. They enjoy their children but feel the loneliness that child care in the isolated home imposes. They sometimes speak of the despair that overtakes them as they face the daily routine of endless caring for others with no time for their own needs. The resentment and guilt that build up often create unhappiness.

6   Over a hundred years ago, an English feminist pointed out that there was no good reason to expect that every mother enjoyed, or was even particularly good at, meeting children's daily needs. Harriet Taylor Mill noticed that child rearing in the private home by the mother was coercive. That is, mothers had no choice in the matter because there were no other socially acceptable arrangements. On the one hand, society said it was "natural" for married women to stay at home and care for children. And on the other hand, society refused to employ married women or even educate them so as to fit them for other

---

[1]**bear:** have

[2]**child rearing:** raising or bring up of children

[3]**sustain:** maintain

jobs. If full-time mothering was so natural, she queried,[4] why did it have to be enforced this way? Why were there prejudices and even laws against educating women, and about employing mothers, if they "naturally" took to staying at home with children?

7   Of course, there is nothing natural about any way of raising children, or those ways would not be so varied. Social custom, not nature, determines what mothering means. Well into the eighteenth century, for example, the aristocratic upper classes of Europe sent their infants to wetnurses until they were weaned at three or four. Urban women who worked as silk spinners and artisans did the same. The wetnurse was usually a peasant who had just recently given birth herself and had a nursing baby of her own. She took in one, and sometimes more, babies and nursed them—as women in the preindustrial household did—while carrying out her work and life in the countryside. Ironically,[5] even among the nineteenth-century bourgeoisie—the group from which we inherit the idea that women are chiefly mothers—the reality was quite different from the ideology. Affluent women of this period frequently handed over the care of their children to servants or slaves—the nannies, governesses, and black mammies who did the daily work of mothering.

8   Men's participation in child care also varies in different cultures and different eras. In tribal societies, a network of female and male kin often care for each others' children. They are all "daughters" and "sons," looked after by the entire group. Among the Arapesh of New Guinea, Margaret Mead observed that the father as well as the mother stays with the infant and meets its momentary needs. Both father and mother are held responsible for child care by the entire community. Indeed, she goes on to say, "if one comments upon a middle-aged man as good-looking, the people answer: 'Good-looking? Ye-e-s? But you should have seen him before he bore[6] all those children.'"

9   What? Men give birth? That may be a little too remote from our experience, although several societies have such notions. What is familiar from our preindustrial period, however, is that fathers were closely involved in the daily work of raising children. The father's role in the preindustrial household included teaching and disciplining. He particularly trained the boys of the household in their future work skills. When fathers left the home to work in factories and offices, the sexual division of labor with regard to child rearing was sharpened. Compulsory schooling took over many of the father's tasks. This brought the benefit of literacy to children, but it meant that fathers lost control over training the boys of the family. It also meant that care of younger children fell almost entirely to women, especially to mothers, who were becoming ever more isolated as everyone else left the home each day for school or for wage work.

10   We can see how out of these historical developments—the introduction of wage work and the division of family labor—our image of the ideal family arose. Daddy leaves the home to go work. Mommy stays home cooking and cleaning. And there are Dick and Jane at school, learning skills and attitudes that will fit them for the work their mothers and fathers do. Or will it? If we take what we know about families, that family structures can be and have been different both historically and from one

[4]**queried:** asked
[5]**ironically:** conveying the opposite meaning
[6]**bore:** gave birth to

society to another, and we piece that information together as if it were an enormous puzzle, we will see an expanded picture that does not fit the roles these children are learning. We will see the full picture of an evolving family structure that is constantly changing, and we will be prepared for the new family that meets the needs of our modern world.

After You Read

• Inferencing to Understand the Main Idea

DIRECTIONS: Choose the answer that best completes the sentence. You will need to make inferences (draw conclusions) about the author's message as you did in unit 3.

1.   According to the author, the many variations in the way people raise children prove that

_____ a.   women are naturally best suited to raise children.

_____ b.   men, such as the Arapesh, do a better job raising children than do women.

_____ c.   social custom rather than nature is the factor which determines who does the child raising.

2.   The author explains, in length, the details of the responsibilities women have in the home to help the reader see that

_____ a.   housework is varied.

_____ b.   housework and child rearing can be frustrating.

_____ c.   women are capable individuals.

3.   The author includes the detail about Harriet Taylor Mill to show that

_____ a.   women should be allowed to attend school.

_____ b.   society forced women to stay at home.

_____ c.   women "naturally" are best suited to work in the home.

4. In the author's view, aristocratic upper-class women in the eighteenth century

    _____ a.   were liberated for sending their children to wetnurses.

    _____ b.   did not enjoy raising children.

    _____ c.   are an example of how social custom varies in childrearing practices.

5. The author believes that history

    _____ a.   explains how women's responsibilities at home evolved.

    _____ b.   shows that women have always had the responsibility of raising children.

    _____ c.   should teach us that our modern societies' values are the same as those of earlier societies.

• Understanding Vocabulary Through Word Analysis

As you learned in unit 3, we can better guess at the meaning of some words if we analyze word parts. Often the endings of words let us know how a word functions in a sentence. One class of words, *adjectives*, can be easily recognized by the word ending called a *suffix*. Common adjective endings are *-able*, *-ous*, *-ive*, *-ory*, and *-ary*. In fact, these word endings rarely occur in other kinds of words. Certain other suffixes found at the end of adjectives, however, can be deceiving. Endings such as *-ing*, *-ed*, and *-ly* can be found at the end of verbs, adverbs, or even nouns.

DIRECTIONS: Locate the following adjectives in the passage. Use context clues and your understanding that these words are adjectives to guess at their meanings. Use a dictionary to find the meanings you cannot guess. Write a synonym or definition for each word in the space provided.

industrialized _____

contemporary _____

orderly _____

satisfying _____

monotonous _____

rewarding _____

imaginative _____

conflicting _____

isolated _____

coercive _____

compulsory _____

In paragraphs 3 and 5 locate words ending in -ing that are *not* adjectives. Determine what part of speech they are, and define the words which are unfamiliar to you.

Example: paragraph 3, line 3: *rearing*—noun meaning "raising."

The Second Reading

As You Read: Understanding the Author's Plan

In your second reading of the passage, locate the thesis statement and write it in the space provided.

_____

_____

_____

_____

Could you guess what the author was going to write about from the thesis statement? Did she fulfill her promise to her readers? To answer this last question, you need to consider the main idea of each paragraph and how it relates to the thesis statement.

DIRECTIONS: In the space provided, write a phrase to describe the main idea of each paragraph. Paragraph 1 serves as an introduction.

Paragraph 2 _____

Paragraph 3 _____

Paragraph 4 _____

Paragraph 5 _____

Paragraph 6 _____

Paragraph 7 _____

Paragraph 8 _____

Paragraph 9 _____

Paragraph 10 _____

After You Read

● Recognizing Paragraph Hooks

In lesson 1 you began looking at cohesive devices, words or phrases that help the reader to see the relationship between the ideas in a paragraph. These devices help to make sentences and ideas "stick" together. In a well-organized essay, a writer will employ similar techniques *between paragraphs*. The use of such devices, called **paragraph hooks,** helps the reader to see the relationship of one paragraph to the next. Paragraph hooks increase the reader's understanding of the passage by encouraging the reader to remember what the major train of thought of the passage is, how one paragraph is related to the thesis. The "hook" often occurs in the first sentence of each paragraph.

Let's look at how Joan Kelly does this in the article you have just read. A strong paragraph hook occurs in paragraph 4. She starts off with,

"Add child care to housework, and we begin to see why the job of 'housewife,' according to a study...."

Without referring back to the previous paragraph, make a guess as to what the last paragraph was about. Now, check your guess against your answers in the last exercise (p. 140). Did you guess right? Paragraph 3 is about housework, and paragraph 4 begins the discussion of child care. By beginning with "Add child care to housework...", the author ties together the first and second parts of the article. She signals a change in topic to the readers and shows how this new idea relates to the last one. Now you can examine the rest of the paragraphs on your own to see how the writer uses other kinds of hooks to make this passage a cohesive piece of writing.

DIRECTIONS: Considering only the first sentence in each paragraph, underline the word or words that act as paragraph hooks in the article, "The Nuclear Family: Women's Work in the Home." Not all of the paragraphs will have hooks. Then determine what the hook refers to in the preceding paragraph. Compare your answers to those of your classmates.

If we compare the thesis statement to the topic sentences of the body paragraphs, we will see that the topic sentence often relates back to the thesis statement. You can find such cohesion in the passage you have been working with in paragraphs 2 and 4.

● Recognizing Transitions

Throughout this unit you have seen the importance of cohesion within individual paragraphs and between paragraphs. Without it, a piece of writing would fall apart as would a house made of bricks with no mortar. Another building block of cohesion that is particularly important *within sentences* is the use of **transition words or phrases. Transitions** fall into three categories:

coordinating conjunctions
subordinating conjunctions, and
introductory adverbs.

Coordinating conjunctions and subordinating conjunctions combine ideas into one sentence. The seven coordinators—*and, but, or, for, nor, so, yet*—combine ideas that are of equal importance. The sentence, "Families differ from society to society, and they have changed over time" (paragraph 1), announces to the reader that the idea of societal differences in families is as important in the passage as is the idea that families have changed.

Subordinating conjunctions (*because, when, if, although*, and so on), on the other hand, make the clause they are connected to less important than the main clause of the sentence. "When fathers left the home to work in factories and offices, the sexual division of labor with regard to child rearing was sharpened" (paragraph 9). This sentence occurs in a paragraph in which the focus is the change in the sexual division of labor, not the fact that fathers left home to work.

Introductory adverbs connect the ideas from one sentence to the next. Paragraphs 5 and 7 in the reading begin with the introductory adverbs *moreover* and *of course*.

The most challenging aspect of learning to use such transitions is knowing the relationship that each word establishes between the ideas it connects. The use of *moreover* in paragraph 5 tells the reader that the fact that many women are not interested in child care is *even more important* than the idea that child care is difficult because it is sometimes in opposition with housekeeping (paragraph 4).

You are already quite familiar with transitions. You have worked with them in unit 3, and you already use many in your writing. The following exercises will help you to increase your awareness of the many different transition words that exist and of how frequently you employ such words in your writing.

DIRECTIONS: With a partner, choose one paragraph in the reading and underline all transition words.

Becoming a Proficient Writer

Guided Writing: Using Transitions

Examine the freewriting you did in lesson 1 for transitions. Rewrite the freewriting, adding transition words when appropriate.

LESSON 3

COMPOSING ON YOUR OWN

The First Draft

Choosing a Topic

DIRECTIONS: Choose one of the following topics to write an essay about. In writing the first draft, you need to focus on getting your ideas on paper without being overly concerned with organization. This, of course, should not prevent you from having some plan in mind as you write.

A. Describe the traditional sex roles assigned to men and women in your society. Explain why you agree or disagree with these assigned roles.
B. Discuss how the sex roles of either men or women have been changing in your society. In your opinion, are these changes for the better or the worse? Why?
C. Choose one of the freewritings you did in lesson 1, and expand it into a full essay which attacks or defends the quotation you had responded to.

Generating Ideas

For either topic A or B, work first on idea generation. Try brainstorming, freewriting, looping, or any techniques that work for you. For topic C, you have already done one freewriting, so consider doing a few loops to generate more ideas on the topic.

Writing the First Draft

After fully examining your topic through idea-generating techniques, start writing. Remember that an open and creative effort at this very important stage of the process will assure you of an interesting final product.

Revising

As always, you need to consider your first draft for content and development. Whether you do this on your own or with a partner, here are a few basic questions that you should address before you continue with your second draft. You might have other questions you would like to address as well. Be careful, however, to examine only the aspects of *content* at this stage.

1. Does your draft clearly have an audience and a purpose?
2. Is your message worthwhile and interesting?
3. Do you include enough relevant detail to convince your audience that your message is valid?

Revise your paper as necessary.

The Second Draft

Once you have revised your first draft in terms of content and development, it is time to go back and consider what you have written in terms of the essay organization concepts you have been working with in the past three units. This would be a good time to review the material covered in these last units. A review will remind you that each paragraph will be easily understood if you employ topic sentences, general to specific organization, and cohesion between sentences. You will also be reminded that your essay should have an introduction, a thesis statement, a clear plan, and paragraph hooks between paragraphs. Make any necessary changes on your paper.

One final element of essay organization that you should consider is the **conclusion.** The following section will help you to write effective conclusions.

Writing an Effective Conclusion

A genuine conclusion is a natural outgrowth from the rest of a well-organized paper. It should give a piece of writing a finished "feeling," and your readers should feel satisfied that the writer has brought the passage to a close.

Conclusions give the writer a chance to sum up the main points of the paper and, then, convince the readers for one last time that the thesis is valid. This final opportunity to "drive home" the main idea of the piece can take many forms. For example, it could be a solution to the problem presented by the thesis, a prediction of future consequences, or an appeal to the readers to take some action. Whatever form this final message takes, it should present a broader view of the issue, a view that leaves the readers with the sense that the message was relevant to them.

When writing a conclusion, consider the following questions.

1. Did you refer to the main idea(s) of the essay, being careful not to restate the thesis?
2. Did you go one step further with the idea of the thesis, being careful not to introduce new ideas that need further explanation?
3. Did you leave your reader feeling satisfied that the essay was worthwhile and that your message had come to a natural conclusion?

Now try to answer these questions for the conclusion of the article in lesson 2. You can do the same for the conclusions in the articles in units 4 and 5. Notice, in particular, how the author of *Ultra Sports* (unit 4, lesson 2) smoothly ends the article by referring back to certain ideas from the introduction.

Once you have examined several examples of effective conclusions, you can try your hand at writing a conclusion to the paper you are working on.

Peerediting for Organization

DIRECTIONS: Choose someone in your class whom you have never worked with before as your partner for this peerediting session. After you have read each other's papers, answer the following questions about your partner's paper. Finally, discuss the answers to the questions for both papers. Keep in mind that it is not too late to make improvements in content as well.

1. Does the introduction attract your interest? If so, what aspect of it appeals to you?

_____

_____

2. Underline the thesis statement. What do you expect the paper to be about?

_____

_____

_____

3. Write the purpose of each body paragraph.

_____

_____

_____

_____

4. Circle the paragraph hooks.

5. Locate transitions within the paragraphs. Are there enough? Are there too many?

6. Locate examples of showing. Are they relevant to the main idea of the essay?

7. Are there parts of the essay that should be expanded with more detail? What detail should be added to make the main idea of the essay better supported?

_____

_____

_____

_____

8. Answer the questions in the preceding exercise about the conclusion of the essay. Was the conclusion successful?

9. What is your favorite part of this essay? Why?

_____

_____

_____

Revising and Writing the Second Draft

By now you have had many experiences revising your papers. You are beginning to get an idea of what makes a good essay through your own revisions and through the feedback that you have given to your classmates and gotten from them and your teacher. Now it is time to look at ways that you can become increasingly your own judge of your work. One very important ability good writers have is being able to look at their own work objectively. If you can distance yourself from what you have written, you can look at your work from the eyes of a reader. You can see what aspects of your writing need additional information to make the message more clear or more convincing.

Although this is a difficult task, there are things that you can do to help you achieve this distance. One technique that might help you to look at your own writing objectively is to use a checklist, like the peerediting guidelines that you just used. Another thing you can do is have someone read your paper to you aloud or listen to a recording you have made of your essay. One final tactic you can use is to let a few days lapse between work sessions so that when you return to work on your paper you view it with "new eyes."

DIRECTIONS: Follow these steps to revise. If possible, give yourself several days for this process.

1. After making corrections on your paper based on your peerediting session, make a brief checklist of further considerations you wish to address. (Don't forget the importance of cohesion.)

2. Go through your paper, answering the questions on your checklist. Make any necessary changes.

3. If possible, record your paper on an audiotape. Then wait a day or two. If you were able to record your essay, listen to the recording without looking at your paper. If not, have someone else read it to you.

4. As you listen to your paper, take notes on any changes you would like to make.

5. Finally, revise one last time.

If your changes are major, rewriting at this point would help to clarify the revisions you have made and any changes that still need to be made.

Proofreading

In this unit you were asked to consider elements of cohesion in your essay. Several of these elements can be looked at grammatically. Following are questions relating to the use of cohesive devices. This should be part of your proofreading process for this essay. This does not mean, of course, that these are the only grammatical aspects of your paper you should consider. You are beginning to know what your individual weaknesses are; make sure that you address those issues as well. Remember to read first for mistakes that you can hear.

DIRECTIONS: After considering your essay for your individual grammatical weaknesses, check your paper for cohesion.

1. Locate transition words that you used to combine ideas. Check to make sure the meaning of the word or phrase expresses the relationship between the ideas. (Did you overuse *and*?) Check to make sure the sentence is correctly punctuated.

2. Locate instances in which you used pronouns, demonstrative pronouns, and demonstrative adjectives. Determine what they refer to, and check to see if you used the appropriate word.

3. Consider subject-verb agreement and verb tense. Is the tense consistent? Does it convey the meaning better than another tense? Did you use the present when another tense would have made your meaning more clear? If there were shifts in time zone, did you announce those changes with a signal word?

Sharing Your Writing

One way of learning how to write successfully is to look at essays that are well written. Throughout this text you have been reading articles that are, in a variety of ways, good examples of writing. Now you will have a chance to look at one or several good pieces of writing that have been done by students. Your teacher will distribute copies of one or more completed student essays from this or the previous unit. As a class, discuss the essay(s). You can refer to the peerediting guidelines that you used in this lesson.

Keeping a Journal

1. Describe your ideal mate. How would you and this mate divide shared responsibilities? What would your roles be?
2. Describe your own family or a family that you know well. What are the roles that the adults in the family play? Do you think these roles are the best for the individuals in this family?

UNIT SEVEN

UNLOCKING OUR WONDROUS MIND: PHYSIOLOGY

LESSON 1

WHY DO WE LIKE MUSIC?

About the Selection:

In many of the reading selections in this text we have seen how science is being used to unlock the mysteries of the universe, thus changing our own lives and those of our children. But can science unlock all of our mysteries? Can it answer all of the questions we have about *who* we are and *why* we are the way that we are? In this article written for the *Science 85* magazine, M. Mitchell Waldrop examines current theories and scientific evidence in an attempt to resolve one such unanswered question: Why do humans enjoy and respond to music? Judge for yourself whether he—or science—can truly answer the question he poses.

Before You Read: Exploring Your Own Ideas by Experiencing the Topic

Before we read an article or other selection, it is generally a good idea to consider our own experiences and thoughts on the topic at hand. The following prereading exercise is designed to help you think more about this author's question ("Why do we like music?" *before* you read about his response. What better way is there to consider this question and prepare for the reading than by listening to a piece of music?

DIRECTIONS: Your teacher will play for you a short piece of music. As the music is playing, close your eyes and just listen. Don't think about your class or what you will eat for dinner tonight or what the person sitting next to you is doing. Just listen to the music and let yourself respond.

After you have heard the music, think about the way in which you responded to it. How did it make you feel (happy and energetic? relaxed and content? proud and strong? fearful? sad? angry?)? Were there particular parts you liked and others that you didn't? How did your body respond? Did the music relax and soothe you or was your heart beating so fast and furiously that you could hardly sit still? Did any pictures form in your mind of places or people you know? Did you think about any particular experiences you have had or would like to have?

Take a few minutes now to freewrite about your response to the music.

Now that you have had a chance to listen to the music and write about your response to it, think about *why* you might have responded in the way that you did. Consider the music; consider yourself—your personality, your background, your culture. In the space provided, jot down a few ideas that might explain the reasons for your response.

_____

_____

_____

_____

_____

_____

As You Read: Reading with a Purpose

The title and the first paragraph of this article pose the question for which Waldrop would like to find the answer. As you read, look for the various explanations given as to why we like music and the reasons why Waldrop rejects each explanation.

WHY DO WE LIKE MUSIC?
by M. Mitchell Waldrop

SALIERI: It started simply enough: just a pulse in the lowest registers—bassons and basset horns—like a rusty squeezebox.... And then suddenly, high above it, sounded a single note on the oboe. It hung there unwavering, piercing me through, till breath could hold it no longer, and a clarinet withdrew it out of me, and sweetened it to a phrase of such delight it had me trembling.

Peter Shaffer, *Amadeus*

1   Music, after all, is nothing more than a sequence of sound waves. So why did the music of Wolfgang Amadeus Mozart fill his rival, Antonio Salieri, with longing and pain? Why do we fill our own lives with music—in the concert halls of Vienna, in the streets of Harlem, on the plains of India? What is it that allows a sequence of sound waves to touch us so deeply?

2   Part of the answer seems to lie in the physics of the sound waves. Scales and chords, for example, are constructed from pitches[1] that are mathematical progressions of one another. When we hear a middle C, the air is vibrating[2] some 260 times per second. Double that to 520 vibrations per second, and we hear a C exactly one octave[3] higher; multiply middle C's vibrations by 3/2, and we hear the G in that octave at 390 vibrations per second.

3   Over the centuries musicians have elaborated such relationships into an enormous body of music theory. But valuable as it is, theory only tells us how music works, not why. It cannot explain why one tune is utterly banal and another is magic.

4   Obviously, a great deal of our appreciation for music is learned. You may like a song that I hate simply because it resembles other songs that you like. On a more fundamental level, the aesthetics[4] of music vary widely between cultures. In the Orient the stress is on pitch and tiny intricate intervals. In sub-Saharan Africa the rhythms reach dizzying complexity. In the 18th-century Europe of Bach and Mozart, the ideal was order, structure, and balance.

5   But again, none of this explains why almost everyone responds to some kind of music, or why music in one form or another appears in every known human society.

6   In the last analysis, it seems that the power of music lies not in the sounds but in ourselves. Just as our eyes are receptors to light and our ears are receptors to sound, we somehow have in our brains a receptor to music. In fact Harvard psychologist Howard Gardner argues that musical intelligence is something that is separate and coequal with other forms of intelligence, such as an ability with words or with numbers.

7   In many ways, Gardner says, music and language abilities are very similar. Babies start to babble fragments of "song" as early as they start to make little word sounds. Older children progress in stages, showing an ability to sing longer and more complex songs in much the same was as they start to use longer and more complex sentences.

[1]**pitch:** the highness or lowness of a musical note
[2]**vibrating:** shaking rapidly
[3]**octave:** a space of 8 degrees between musical notes
[4]**aesthetics:** philosophy or viewpoint concerning what is beautiful in art

8   But music is not just language in another form, says Gardner. For example, the Soviet composer V. Shebalin suffered a stroke[5] in the left temporal lobe[6] of his brain, the area for language comprehension. Afterwards he had great difficulty communicating, yet his compositions were as brilliant and as sensitive as ever.

9   On the other hand, a young musical composer suffered damage to the right hemisphere of his brain. He had no trouble communicating and eventually returned to teaching music. But he had lost all interest in composition. He even lost much of his enjoyment in listening to music.

10   Studies such as these, Gardner says, indicate that some key essence of our musicality is located in the right front of the brain. The exact location, however, and the exact nature of that essence is far from clear. Even if we do someday track down the brain's "music receptor," we are still left with one final mystery: Why is it there? Some scholars have suggested that our musical abilities evolved at the same time we acquired language, anywhere from a few hundred thousands years ago to a million years ago. Yet language gave our tribal ancestors a clear evolutionary advantage: Better communication meant a better chance at survival. What need did music serve?

11   Of course, we would also ask that question about painting or sculpture, dance or poetry. Why do humans respond to beauty of any kind? To that question, we have no more answer than Shaffer's tortured Salieri, who cried up to his 'sharp old God': What is this? Tell me, Signore! What is this pain? What is this need in the sound? Forever unfulfillable, yet fulfilling him who hears it, utterly."

[5]**stroke:** a break or blockage of a blood vessel in the brain
[6]**left temporal lobe:** the section of the brain near the left temple (front)

M. Mitchell Waldrop, "Why do we like music?" *Science 85* magazine, March 1985. Copyright © 1985 M. Mitchell Waldrop. Reprinted by permission of the author.

After You Read

• Recalling Information

DIRECTIONS: Following is a list of statements about music and our appreciation of it. To the left of each statement are two letters, *T* and *F*. Without referring back to the article, try to determine whether the statement is true or false. If the statement is true according to the information in the article, circle *T*. If it is false, circle *F*.

T F 1. By understanding the physics of the sound waves, we will understand *why* people respond to music in the way they do.

T F 2. Much of our appreciation for different types of music is learned.

T F 3. Although in most cultures music is very important, in some human societies there is little or no music at all.

T F 4. We are usually attracted to and like music that is very different from what we are used to.

T F 5. According to the author, human beings respond to music mainly because we have a special "music receptor" in our brain.

T   F   6.   Music ability and language ability seem to develop in children at approximately the same time.

T   F   7.   Because of the similarities between music ability and language ability, most scientists believe that music is really language in another form.

T   F   8.   When scientists discover the exact location of the brain's "music receptor," the mystery of why we like music will finally be solved.

● Comprehending the Reading: Making Inferences

When we infer meaning from a reading passage, we need to be certain that the conclusions we draw are adequately supported by the information the author has provided. The following activity takes you beyond the inferencing exercises of units 3 and 6. The choices contain not only statements that are false according to the reading, but also conclusions that require more information than the passage offers. To respond to this activity, you will need to consider carefully how the information included in the passage leads to certain conclusions.

DIRECTIONS: Read over the paragraph indicated for each group of statements. Then read each statement. If the statement is an inference which can reasonably be drawn from the information in the paragraph, put an X in the space provided to the left. If the statement cannot be concluded from the paragraph, leave the space blank. Be prepared to justify your answers. Paragraph 4 has been done for you as an example.

Paragraph 4: Example

_____   a.   People must be taught to like music.

____X____   b.   Our taste in music is influenced by our culture.

_____   c.   The author believes that a good piece of music will be equally appreciated by people of all cultural backgrounds.

____X____   d.   Different cultures seem to emphasize different aspects of music.

Paragraph 4: Explanation
a.   This statement is an incorrect interpretation of the first sentence in the paragraph and is contradicted by the information in paragraph 7.
b.   This can be inferred from the statement "the aesthetics of music vary widely between cultures" and from the examples given in the paragraph.
c.   This statement seems to contradict the information given in the paragraph regarding the varying aesthetics between cultures.
d.   This conclusion is apparent from the examples given in the paragraph.

Paragraph 8

_____   a.   Psychologist Howard Gardner believes that music and language have the same form.

_____ b.   Shebalin's stroke affected his ability to communicate because it occurred in the part of the brain that governs language comprehension.

_____ c.   Shebalin's stroke affected his composing ability.

_____ d.   Shebalin's stroke did not damage the part of the brain that governs musical ability.

_____ e.   We can infer that Shebalin's music ability and his language ability were not located in the same place in his brain.

Paragraph 9

_____ a.   The stroke suffered by the young composer referred to in this paragraph occurred in a different part of the brain from that of Shebalin.

_____ b.   This composer's musical ability and interest were damaged by the stroke.

_____ c.   The damage to this composer's language ability eventually healed.

_____ d.   Teaching music does not require an interest in composition.

_____ e.   This composer began teaching music after his stroke because he could no longer compose.

_____ f.   The stroke affected his appreciation of music but did not affect his ability to communicate.

Paragraphs 8 and 9

_____ a.   We can infer from these two paragraphs that an individual's musical and linguistic abilities are governed from different parts of the brain.

_____ b.   The examples given contradict Gardner's statement that music and language ability are very similar.

_____ c.   The examples suggest that a person's musical ability (music receptor) is located in the left half of the brain and language ability is located in the right half.

Paragraph 10

_____ a.   Scientists will someday track down the exact location of the brain's "music receptor."

_____ b.   Human beings' music abilities evolved along with our ability to use language, thus increasing early humans' chance for survival.

_____ c.   The author does not know what need music served early humans.

_____ d.   The author believes that when we find the music receptor, we'll have solved the mystery of why we like music.

Inferencing is an important skill to acquire. When we read, our inferences help us to comprehend the author's message more fully and relate it to our own experiences. When we write, we use our inferencing skills to examine the logic on which our conclusions have been based while we construct a passage in which we lead our reader to similar conclusions. Our discussion of logical fallacies in unit 8 is related to inferencing.

Becoming a Proficient Writer

Listen, Respond, and Write

Now that you've been introduced to some ideas about why we like music and about the relationship between music and language, listen again to the music your teacher played for you at the beginning of this lesson. This time, however, write about your responses and your thoughts *while* you are listening to the piece rather than afterwards.

Sharing Your Ideas

DIRECTIONS: First read over your two written responses to the music you heard. Then, as a class or in small groups, discuss the following questions.

1.   What was your general response to the music? Did you like it or dislike it? Did you enjoy some parts of the piece and not enjoy others? If so, which ones? Did you form any particular images in your mind as you listened? Compare your responses with those of your classmates, and discuss possible reasons for any differences you might have.

2.   Did your response to or feelings about the music change at all when you listened to it a second time? If so, how? Can you suggest any reasons for this change?

3.   The first time you heard the music, you wrote about your response *after* you listened to it; the second time you did your writing *while* the music was playing. Did this difference change either your feeling about the writing process or your response to the music? If so, how? What possible reasons for the change does the reading suggest?

LESSON 2

YOUR BRAIN: THE RIGHT AND LEFT OF IT

About the Selection

In the previous lesson, you read about efforts to locate what Waldrop called the "music receptor" in the brain. These efforts are based on the theory that different portions of the brain serve different purposes. In her book *Drawing on the Right Side of the Brain*, artist-professor Betty Edwards explores how this theory of the brain relates to artistic perception in general and to the skill of drawing in particular. Chapter 3 of her book (excerpted here) discusses the two hemispheres of the brain and the ways in which each perceives and interprets reality. This chapter lays the theoretical foundation for Dr. Edwards's popular and highly successful method for teaching drawing skills.

The First Reading

As You Read: Looking for the Main Idea

As you read through the selection the first time, keep in mind the following general questions, as they will help you to identify the main point of the article.

1. What new discovery did scientists make about the two sides of the brain in the 1960s?
2. According to today's scientists, how do the two hemispheres of the brain differ?
3. What kind of evidence does Dr. Edwards use to support her discussion of the "double brain"?

YOUR BRAIN: THE RIGHT AND LEFT OF IT
by Dr. Betty Edwards

"Every creative act involves... a new innocence of perception, liberated from the cataract of accepted belief."
—Arthur Koestler, *The Sleepwalkers*

[1]   A creative person is one who can process in new ways the information directly at hand—the ordinary sensory data[1] available to all of us. A writer needs words, a musician needs notes, an artist needs visual perceptions, and all need some knowledge of the techniques of their crafts. But a creative individual intuitively[2] sees possibilities for transforming ordinary data into a new creation.

[2]   Time and again, creative individuals have recognized the differences between the two processes of gathering data and transforming those data creatively. Recent discoveries about how the brain works are beginning to illuminate[3] that dual process.

Getting to Know Both Sides of Your Brain

[3]   Seen from above, the human brain resembles the halves of a walnut—two similar appearing, convoluted, rounded halves connected at the center (Figure A). The two halves are called the "left hemisphere" and the "right hemisphere."

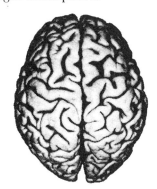

Figure A

[1]**sensory data:** information received through the five senses (sight, hearing, touch, smell, taste)
[2]**intuitively:** through direct insight; without using reason or logic
[3]**illuminate:** make clear

[4] The human nervous system is connected to the brain in a crossed-over fashion. The left hemisphere controls the right side of the body, the right hemisphere controls the left side. If you suffer a stroke or accidental brain damage to the left half of your brain, for example, the right half of your body will be most seriously affected and vice versa. Because of this crossing over of the nerve pathways, the left hand is connected to the right hemisphere; the right hand, to the left hemisphere, as shown in Figure B.

The Double Brain

[5] In the brains of animals, the cerebral hemispheres (the two halves of the brain) are essentially alike, or symmetrical, in function. Human cerebral hemispheres, however, develop asymmetrically in terms of function. The most noticeable outward effect of the asymmetry of the human brain is handedness.

[6] For the past one-hundred fifty years or so, scientists have known that the function of language and language-related capabilities is mainly located in the left hemispheres of the majority of individuals—approximately 98 percent of right-handers and about two thirds of left-handers. Knowledge that the left half of the brain is specialized for language functions was largely derived from observations of the effects of brain injuries. It was apparent, for example, that an injury to the left side of the brain was more likely to cause a loss of speech capability than an injury of equal severity to the right side.

[7] Because speech and language are so closely linked to thinking, reasoning, and

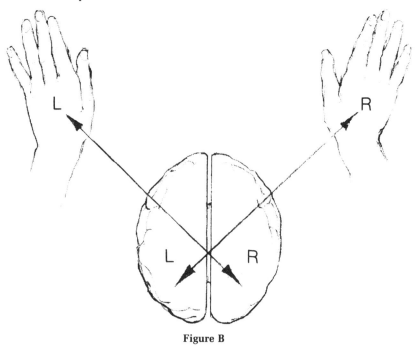

The crossover connections of left-hand to right-hemisphere, right-hand to left-hemisphere.

Figure B

the higher mental functions that set human beings apart from the other creatures of the world, nineteenth-century scientists named the left hemisphere the dominant or *major* hemisphere; the right brain, the subordinate or *minor* hemisphere. The general view, which prevailed until fairly recently, was that the right half of the brain was less advanced, less evolved than the left half—a mute[4] twin with lower-level capabilities, directed and carried along by the verbal[5] left hemisphere.

[8]   Then during the 1960s, studies on human neurosurgical patients provided further information on the function of the corpus callosum [the thick nerve cable which connects the two hemispheres—see Figure C] and caused scientists to postulate a revised view of the relative capabilities of the halves of the human brain: that both hemispheres are involved in higher cognitive functioning, with each half of the brain specialized in complementary fashion for different *modes* of thinking, both highly complex.

[9]   Because this changed perception of the brain has important implications for education in general and for learning to draw in particular, I'll briefly describe some of the research often referred to as the "split-brain" studies. The research was mainly carried out at Cal Tech by Sperry and his students Michael Gazzaniga, Jerre Levy, Colwyn Travarthen, Robert Nebes, and others.

[10]   The investigation centered on a small group of individuals who came to be known as "split-brain" patients. They are persons who had been greatly disabled by epileptic seizures that involved both hemispheres.

[4]**mute:** silent
[5]**verbal:** using words and language

A diagram of one half of a human brain, showing the corpus callosum and related commissures.

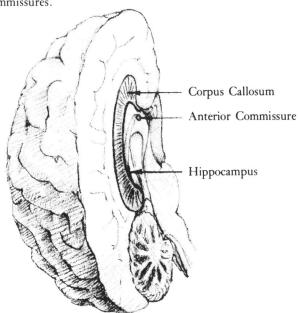

Corpus Callosum

Anterior Commissure

Hippocampus

Figure C

After all other remedies had failed, the spread of seizures between the two hemispheres was controlled by means of an operation, performed by Phillip Vogel and Joseph Bogen, that severed the corpus callosum and the related or cross-connections thus isolating one hemisphere from the other. The operation yielded the hoped-for result: the patients' seizures were controlled and they regained health. In spite of the radical nature of the surgery, the patients' outward appearance, manner, and coordination were little affected; and to casual observation their ordinary daily behavior seemed little changed.

11   The Cal Tech group subsequently worked with these patients in a series of ingenious[6] and subtle[7] tests that revealed the separated functions of the two hemispheres. The tests provided surprising new evidence that each hemisphere, in a sense, perceives its own reality—or perhaps better stated, perceives reality in its own way. The verbal half of the brain—the left half—dominates most of the time in individuals with intact brains as well as in the split-brain patients. Using ingenious procedures, however, the Cal Tech group tested the patients' separated right hemispheres and found evidence that the right, nonspeaking half of the brain also experiences, responds with feelings, and processes information on its own. In our own brains, with intact corpora callosa, communication between the hemispheres melds or reconciles the two perceptions, thus preserving our sense of being one person, a unified being.

12   In addition to studying the right/left separation of inner mental experience, the scientists examined the different ways in which the two hemispheres process in-formation. Evidence accumulated[8] showing that the mode of the left hemisphere is verbal and analytic,[9] while that of the right is nonverbal and global.[10] New evidence found by Jerre Levy in her doctoral studies showed that the mode of processing used by the right brain is rapid, complex, whole-pattern, spatial, and perceptual—processing that is not only different from but comparable in complexity to the left brain's verbal, analytic mode. Additionally, Levy found indications that the two modes of processing tend to interfere with each other, preventing maximal performance; and she suggested that this may be a rationale for the evolutionary development of asymmetry in the human brain—as a means of keeping the two different modes of processing in two different hemispheres.

13   Based on the evidence of the split-brain studies, the view came gradually that *both* hemispheres use high-level cognitive modes which, though different, involve thinking, reasoning, and complex mental functioning. Over the past decade, since the first statement in 1968 by Levy and Sperry, scientists have found extensive supporting evidence for this view, not only in brain-injured patients but also in individuals with normal, intact brains.

14   As a result of these extraordinary findings over the past fifteen years, we now know that despite our normal feeling that we are one person—a single being—our brains are double, each half with its own way of knowing, its own way of perceiving external reality. In a manner of speaking, each of us has two minds, two consciousnesses, mediated and integrated by the connecting cable of nerve fibers between the hemispheres.

[6]**ingenious:** clever
[7]**subtle:** fine or delicate in meaning; difficult to perceive or distinguish
[8]**accumulated:** was collected or gathered together; increased
[9]**analytic:** figuring things out step-by-step and part-by-part
[10]**global:** comprehensive; perceiving the *whole* thing rather than the *parts*

[15] We have learned that the two hemispheres can work together in a number of ways. Sometimes they cooperate with each half contributing its special abilities and taking on the particular part of the task that is suited to its mode of information processing. At other times, the hemispheres can work singly; with one half "on," the other half more or less "off." And it seems that the hemispheres may also conflict, one half attempting to do what the other half "knows" it can do better. Furthermore, it may be that each hemisphere has a way of keeping knowledge from the other hemisphere. It may be, as the saying goes, that the right hand truly does not know what the left hand is doing.

From *Drawing on the Right Side of the Brain* by Betty Edwards. Jeremy P. Tarcher, Inc., Los Angeles and Souvenir Press Ltd., London. Copyright © 1979 by Betty Edwards.

After You Read

● Understanding the Main Idea

DIRECTIONS: Choose the correct answer(s) for the following questions. (Note: More than one answer may be correct. Indicate all the correct answers for each question.)

1. What discovery concerning the two hemispheres of the brain did scientists make in the 1960s?
    a.   The right hemisphere is dominant in most people.
    b.   The left hemisphere controls language-related capabilities.
    c.   Each hemisphere has a specialized, complex mode of thinking.
2. In what way(s) does the functioning of the two hemispheres differ?
    a.   The left hemisphere is more advanced and complex than the right.
    b.   The right hemisphere controls the left side of the body, and the left hemisphere controls the right side.
    c.   The mode of the left hemisphere is analytical and verbal; the mode of the right hemisphere is global and nonverbal.
3. What evidence does Dr. Edwards use to support her discussion of the two hemispheres?
    a.   quotes from famous scientists
    b.   research studies on neurosurgical patients
    c.   anecdotes (stories) of individual "split-brain" patients

● Understanding Vocabulary from Context

DIRECTIONS: For questions 1 through 4, read the paragraphs indicated to find the identified words. Use the context of the sentence and paragraph to guess the meaning of each word. Write your guess (a synonym or explanation of the word in that context) in the space provided. Then identify and write the clues you used to arrive at your guess. (These may be other key words, punctuation, grammatical clues, parts of the words, and so on.)

1. In paragraph 5, what do the words *symmetrical* and *asymmetrically* mean?

   symmetrical: _____

   clues: _____

   asymmetrically: _____

   clues: _____

2. In paragraph 7:

   dominant: _____

   clues: _____

   subordinate: _____

   clues: _____

3. In paragraph 8:

   postulate: _____

   clues: _____

   cognitive functioning: _____

   clues: _____

   modes: _____

   clues: _____

4. In paragraph 12:

   rationale: _____

   clues: _____

5. Notice that the italicized words in the following sentences appear to have similar meanings based on the similarity of the contexts. Use this context to arrive at a guess

about their general meaning. Then look up each word in your dictionary to discover the differences between them.

"In our own brains, with intact corpora callosa, communication between the two hemispheres *melds* or *reconciles* the two perceptions, thus preserving our sense of being one person." (paragraph 11)

"Each of us has two minds, two consciousnesses, *mediated* and *integrated* by the connecting cable of nerve fibers between the hemispheres." (paragraph 14)

General guess: _____
Dictionary meanings:

    meld: _____

    reconcile: _____

    mediated: _____

    integrated: _____

The Second Reading

As You Read: Understanding the Author's Plan

As you read through the selection a second time, look for the author's overall plan of organization, as this will help you to understand the particular points she included about the brain's functioning. Pay particular attention to Dr. Edwards's use of research evidence as support for her conclusions. This method of support is very common in academic writing, and Dr. Edwards's summary of the research studies follows a typical pattern with which you should become familiar.

After You Read

● Recognizing the Author's Plan

DIRECTIONS: Identify the paragraphs which fulfill the following purposes in the article.

a. Interest the reader and identify
the topic of the article
(Underline the thesis statement.)   Paragraph(s) _____

b. Give a brief introduction to the
two sides of the brain   Paragraph(s) _____

c. Provide historical background
concerning our understanding   Paragraph(s) _____

d. Present the modern view of the
    two hemispheres   Paragraph(s) _____

e. Present research studies to
    support the modern view   Paragraph(s) _____

f. Conclude by presenting a general
    picture of how the hemispheres
    work together and independently   Paragraph(s) _____

● Recognizing the Use of Research Evidence

Just as showing details and statistics can be used to support an idea the author wants to communicate, so can various types of research evidence provide a basis for believing the author's conclusions are valid. Some of the following questions ask you to find and write down the evidence that Betty Edwards uses to support her points.

DIRECTIONS: Write the answers to the following questions about the reading selection. Check your answers with your classmates' answers.

1. How is the human "double brain" different from that of other animals?

2. How did early scientists learn that language-related abilities are located in the left hemisphere of the brain?

3. What is the role of the corpus callosum?

4. Underline the sentence in paragraph 8 that identifies the modern view of the two hemispheres. In what ways is this view different from that of the nineteenth-century scientists?

5. Notice that paragraphs 9–13 focus on research evidence to support this modern view. The following questions refer to this research.

    a. What information does paragraph 9 present about the research?

    b. What information does paragraph 10 summarize? Did the subjects in the study undergo surgery for the purpose of Sperry's experiments? If not, what was the reason for their surgery?

    c. What general information did the Cal Tech group learn from their tests? What did they learn about the left hemisphere? About the right hemisphere? About the corpora callosa?

    d. What two main conclusions did Jerre Levy's evidence lead to?

    e. Notice that the first sentence of paragraph 13 again states the general conclusion drawn from the experiments. What is the purpose of the last statement of this paragraph?

6. In recent years, some people have used the research on cerebral hemispheres to classify individuals as being either "right-brained" or "left-brained." Based on paragraphs 14 and 15, do you think that Betty Edwards would agree with these classifications? Why or why not?

● Recognizing and Using Comparative Structures

Because Betty Edwards's purpose in this chapter is to compare the two hemispheres of the brain, a number of grammatical structures commonly used to show similarities and differences emerge in her writing. Several sentences containing these structures are excerpted from the chapter and explained here. Please note that these examples contain only a few of the many common ways to demonstrate contrast and similarity in English.

DIRECTIONS: Briefly answer the following questions in the space provided.

A. Showing similarity or difference within a clause

Pattern 1: Combined subject

   1. "In the brains of animals, the cerebral hemispheres are essentially alike..."

   2. "...both hemispheres use high-level cognitive modes..."

What is being compared in 1? _____

in 2? _____

Notice that the two things being compared function together as the subject of each sentence.

What key word in 1 identifies that the compared items are similar?

_____

What key word in 2 signals the similarity? _____

This pattern of placing the items to be compared or contrasted in the subject of the sentence is one grammatical structure used in comparative sentences.

> **Pattern: A + B are similar.**

Pattern 2: Single subject

   3. "The right half of the brain was less advanced, less evolved than the left."
   4. "...The mode of processing used by the right brain... is not only different from but comparable to the left brain's verbal, analytical mode."

What two things are being contrasted in 3? _____

Which of these is in the subject to the sentence? _____

Where in the sentence is the other item being contrasted? _____

Do you see a similar pattern in 4? _____

What is the subject of the sentence? _____

What is it being compared to? _____

> **Pattern: A is similar to B.**
> **A is different from B.**

COMPARING/CONTRASTING TERMS TO USE *WITHIN* A CLAUSE			
Subject = A + B	Example	Subject = A	Example

1. A and B are the same
     alike
     similar
     comparable
	Painting and
	photography
	are similar.
		1. A is the same as B
		   A is similar to B
		   A resembles B
		   A is like B
			Painting resembles
			photography.

2. Both A and B are _____ Neither A nor B is _____	Both painting and photography are art forms.	2. A is as _____ as B	Painting is as creative as photography.

3. A and B are different
     unlike
     dissimilar
	Painting and
	photography are
	different.
		3. A differs from B
		   A is different from B
		   A is more/less/-er than B
			Painting is messier
			than photography.

B. Showing similarity or difference between clauses

1. "In the brains of animals, the cerebral hemispheres are essentially alike.... Human cerebral hemispheres, however, develop asymmetrically."

What is being contrasted in the two sentences? _____
Notice that one element of the contrast is in the first sentence, and the other is in the second sentence.

What transition word signals the contrast? _____

2. "...the mode of the left hemisphere is verbal and analytical while that of the right is nonverbal and global."

What is being compared? _____   _____

What subordinator signals the contrast between the subjects of these two

clauses? _____

JOINING/TRANSITION WORDS TO USE *BETWEEN* CLAUSES & SENTENCES			
	coordinators	subordinators	transition words
similarity:	and		likewise similarly also too
difference:	but (yet)	while whereas although/though even though	however in contrast conversely on the other hand

(Note: See unit 6, lesson 2 for an explanation of these structures and how to use them.)

Note: You can compare only *logically equivalent* concepts.

For example: (wrong) "The right hemisphere's *mode of thinking* is as complex as the *left hemisphere*."

The preceding sentence incorrectly compares a mode of thinking to an entire hemisphere of the brain. The correct comparison would be between one mode of thinking and another mode of thinking.

Expressions to correct this problem:
that of
the one of
_____'s

For example: (correct) "The right hemisphere's mode of thinking is as complex as *that of* the left hemisphere." (or "... as the left hemisphere's.")

Becoming a Proficient Writer

Guided Writing: Using Comparative Structures

In the following exercise you will have an opportunity to explore further the differences between the right and left hemispheres as you practice the structures of comparison you have just learned.

DIRECTIONS: Using the following chart, write a paragraph contrasting the left and right modes of information processing in the brain. Organize the paragraph so that the two modes are contrasted first in terms of one point (for example, verbal versus nonverbal) then another (for example, analytic versus synthetic) and so on. This is called a point-by-point method of comparison. Include at least five sets of characteristics from the chart, and use a variety of the comparative structures.

A Comparison of Left-Mode and Right-Mode Characteristics

 — MODE

 — MODE

Verbal: Using words to name, describe, define.

Analytic: Figuring things out step-by-step and part-by-part.

Symbolic: Using a symbol to *stand for* something. For example, the drawn form stands for *eye*, the sign + stands for the process of addition.

Abstract: Taking out a small bit of information and using it to represent the whole thing.

Temporal: Keeping track of time, sequencing one thing after another: Doing first things first, second things second, etc.

Rational: Drawing conclusions based on *reason* and *facts*.

Digital: Using numbers as in counting.

Logical: Drawing conclusions based on logic: one thing following another in logical order — for example, a mathematical theorem or a well-stated argument.

Linear: Thinking in terms of linked ideas, one thought directly following another, often leading to a convergent conclusion.

Nonverbal: Awareness of things, but minimal connection with words.

Synthetic: Putting things together to form wholes.

Concrete: Relating to things as they are, at the present moment.

Analogic: Seeing likenesses between things; understanding metaphoric relationships.

Nontemporal: Without a sense of time.

Nonrational: Not requiring a basis of reason or facts; willingness to suspend judgment.

Spatial: Seeing where things are in relation to other things, and how parts go together to form a whole.

Intuitive: Making leaps of insight, often based on incomplete patterns, hunches, feelings, or visual images.

Holistic: Seeing whole things all at once; perceiving the overall patterns and structures, often leading to divergent conclusions.

LESSON 3

COMPOSING
ON YOUR OWN

The First Draft

Choosing a Topic and Generating Ideas

DIRECTIONS: Choose one of the following four topics. We make suggestions in each case for ways to gather your thoughts, but feel free to use whatever idea-generating techniques work well for you and seem appropriate to the topic.

A.   In lesson 1 you heard a piece of music and freewrote about your response to that music. Now, on your own, listen to another musical selection, preferably one of your favorites. Then write a composition comparing the two selections and your reactions to them.

   Suggestions: 1. You may want to listen to the first piece of music again and jot down any observations which you might have missed before. 2. You may want to use the same freewriting technique on your second musical selection that you did on the first. 3. Then, you can compare what you wrote about each selection. You might consider the following questions before you draft your composition: Are there similarities in the two musical pieces? What are the differences? What aspects of the music might you compare (rhythm, tone, instrumentation, complexity, style, and so on)? Were your reactions to the two pieces noticeably different? Why?

B.   Write the same composition as for topic A, but compare two paintings or other pieces of art rather than two musical selections.

Suggestion: Use the same technique explained in topic A. Observe each work of art and freewrite about each.

C.   In the following quotation, Russian scientist Leonid Ponomorev compares the viewpoints (the "modes" of perception) of science and art, arguing that they are different but equally important and complementary aspects of human experience. Write a composition in which you compare the roles of science and art in society.

> It has long been known that science is only one of the methods of studying the world around us. Another—complementary—method is realized in art. The joint existence of art and science is in itself a good illustration of the complementarity principle. You can devote yourself completely to science or live exclusively in your art. Both points of view are equally valid, but, taken separately, are incomplete. The backbone of science is logic and experiment. The basis of art is intuition and insight. But the art of ballet requires mathematical accuracy and, as Pushkin wrote, 'Inspiration in geometry is just as necessary as in poetry.' They complement rather than contradict each other. True science is akin to art, in the same way as real art always includes elements of science. They reflect different, complementary aspects of human experience and give us a complete idea of the world only when taken together.

Suggestion: You may want to brainstorm with other students about the topic before you write. Start by listing the ways in which science and art are used by society; in what contexts are they used and to what ends? Consider your own experience as well as any broader knowledge of history and the social sciences you may have. When your lists are complete, discuss with your classmates how the information might be grouped so that comparable aspects of the two "ways of knowing" might be identified. Based on your discussions, would you agree that the two are complementary aspects of human experience?

D.   Write a composition similar to that of topic C, but focus on the role of art and science in *your* life as an individual rather than in society as a whole.

Suggestion: Try using the same brainstorming technique explained in topic C, but list the ways you use science and art. For example, when you have a problem, do you play a piece of soothing music or take out a set of paints and canvas, or do you immediately sit down to figure out a logical analysis of and solution to the problem? How do you spend your time, both work time and leisure time? What approach do you take to a new experience or idea?

Writing the First Draft and Revising

Use the ideas you have generated to write a draft of your essay. Then examine what you have written for the fullness of the content. You may use the questions for the first draft in unit 6 as guidelines. Make the necessary changes. You may choose to rewrite this draft now if the changes you wish to make are major ones.

The Second Draft

Analyzing the Organization of Comparisons

The organization of your ideas is very important in any kind of comparison because your reader must be able to see what aspects of the subjects are being compared or contrasted at any given time. For this reason, the focus of this revision exercise will be on the organization of your ideas.

DIRECTIONS: After you have completed your first draft and have made some revisions, use the following guidelines to continue your revising process.

1. Read over your draft and construct a flowchart showing how you organized your ideas. (See unit 5 for a review of flowcharts.)
2. Now determine which basic method of organization you used in your composition. There are two main organizational methods used for comparison. One is the point-by-point method you used in the guided writing at the end of lesson 2. The other is the block method in which one subject is discussed in all its relevant aspects and then the other subject is discussed in those same aspects. The two techniques are diagrammed as follows:

POINT-BY-POINT ORGANIZATION

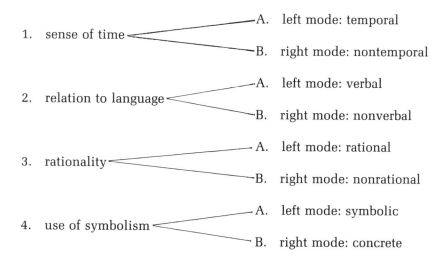

1. sense of time
    A. left mode: temporal
    B. right mode: nontemporal

2. relation to language
    A. left mode: verbal
    B. right mode: nonverbal

3. rationality
    A. left mode: rational
    B. right mode: nonrational

4. use of symbolism
    A. left mode: symbolic
    B. right mode: concrete

BLOCK METHOD OF ORGANIZATION

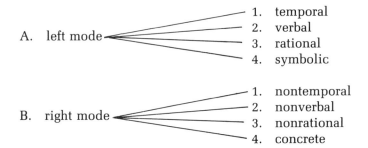

You should be able to tell from a basic flowchart which method of organization you used. Either method is acceptable, but in either case, the information you present for each subject must be ordered clearly. Notice, for example, that in the block method each paragraph covers the same aspects of both subjects in the same order. In the point-by-point method, each point is discussed for subject A first, and for subject B second (not for subject A then subject B on some points and subject B then subject A on others).

3. Now construct flowcharts for the key body paragraphs in your composition. Is the information presented in a clear order? Have you left out any points that you should now include? Make any changes needed in your draft.

Peerediting and Rewriting for Organization

DIRECTIONS: After you have made the needed changes in the organization and development of your ideas, exchange your revised draft with a partner. Then follow these guidelines.

1. Read through your partner's paper once, and note any elements of it that you particularly like. Mention these to your partner. Then go through the paper carefully section by section.
2. The introduction:
    a. Does the introduction catch your interest? Why or why not?
    b. Is there a thesis statement which clearly identifies the topic and intent of the paper?
3. The comparison:
    a. What method of organization does the author use?
    b. Does the author describe both similarities and differences? If so, are these discussed in separate paragraphs? Which is emphasized, the similarities or the differences?
    c. Are the specific points of the comparison relevant to the purpose of the composition? If not, what information should be omitted and what should be added?

     d. Are the specific points of comparison organized clearly and consistently throughout the paper?

     e. Is the author always comparing logically equivalent concepts? If not, locate any flaws in his or her logic.

     f. Discuss with your partner any suggestions you have about how the comparison might be improved.

4. The conclusion:

     a. Does the paper have a conclusion?

     b. Is it relevant to the topic and does it provide a sense of closure to the paper?

     c. Is it interesting? If so, why? If not, how could it be changed?

5. When you have finished, return the paper to its author and discuss the suggestions and comments you each have.

6. Revise/rewrite your paper based on this discussion.

Proofreading

DIRECTIONS: After you have finished the final draft of your paper, proofread your own work. For the purpose of this lesson, focus part of your proofreading on the structures of comparison.

1. Proofread for intuitive knowledge.

2. a. Double check to be sure that the items compared are logically equivalent.

     b. Be sure that you have used the appropriate term of comparison or contrast (including the correct preposition).

     c. If you have used any subordinators or transition words, check to see if your choice of joining word and your punctuation are correct in each case.

3. Proofread for other grammatical errors (verb tense, subject-verb agreement, plural endings, spelling, punctuation).

Sharing Your Writing

    Exchange papers once again with your peerediting partner. Notice the changes you each made in your final drafts. Discuss the strengths and weaknesses of each composition and decide together whether either or both compositions should be shared with the rest of the class.

Keeping a Journal

1. In lesson 1, you freewrote about your reaction as a listener to a particular piece of music. Now change your point of view and consider this music from the perspective of the composer. What do you think his or her purpose was for writing this music? Was he or she trying to communicate an idea or mood? Playing with interesting sounds? Do you sense that there was a particular experience that inspired this piece? If so, describe what that experience might have been.

2. In her conclusion, Betty Edwards says that at some times, "the hemispheres can work singly; with one half 'on,' the other half more or less 'off.'" Think about your daily activities. Describe any of your regular activities for which you might rely on only the right *or* the left hemisphere. What about these activities leads you to believe they use only one mode of perception?

3. Imagine what your life would be like if you could use only one mode of perception all the time—that is, if you could perceive the world *only* in the left mode or *only* in the right. Which mode would you choose as the one which you would most like to keep? Why? Describe how your life would be different without the use of the other mode.

UNIT EIGHT

COPING IN OUR WORLD: PSYCHOLOGY

LESSON 1

WHY WE LAUGH

About the Selection:

In many of the fields that we have considered in this text, we have seen how our modern world is helping us to better understand our environment and ourselves. In the twentieth century, we have begun not only exploring new horizons but also reexamining age-old realities of our present world. One field that has been greatly affected by this reexamination is psychology, where we have begun asking questions about universal human responses. In this next reading, Janet Spencer summarizes scientific research on one such universal human response, laughter. The title of the article announces the theme: "Why We Laugh."

Before You Read: Exploring Your Own Ideas

Think of the last time you laughed heartily. In a freewriting, describe what made you laugh and why it was funny to you. In small groups, share this experience. Then read the article to see if one of the reasons the author gives for laughter seems to explain the reason you laughed in the incident you described.

WHY WE LAUGH
By Janet Spencer

Are you a quiet giggler? Or can you let loose with hearty laughter? Your ability to laugh may mean more than you think.

1   Picture this cartoon: A man is watering his lawn just as an attractive blonde walks by. As he ogles[1] her, he accidentally turns the hose on his dowdy[2] wife, who is sitting on the porch.

2   Men usually think the cartoon is funny. Women do not. And there's a good reason for the difference in opinion.

3   We start finding things laughable—or not laughable—early in life. An infant first smiles at approximately eight days of age. Many psychologists feel this is his first sign of simple pleasure—food, warmth and comfort. At six months or less, the infant laughs to express complex pleasures—such as the sight of Mother's smiling face.

4   In his book *Beyond Laughter,* psychiatrist Martin Grotjahn says that the earlier an infant begins to smile and laugh, the more advanced is his development. Studies revealed that children who did not develop these responses (because they lacked an intimate, loving relationship) "developed a schizophrenic psychosis in later life, or simply gave up and died."

5   Between the ages of six months and one year, the baby learns to laugh for essentially the same reasons he will laugh throughout his life, says Dr. Jacob Levine, associate professor of psychology at Yale University. Dr. Levine says that people laugh to express mastery over an anxiety. Picture what happens when a father tosses his child into the air. The child will probably laugh—but not the first time. In spite of his enjoyment of "flying," he is too anxious to laugh. How does he know Daddy will catch him? Once the child realizes he will be caught, he is free to enjoy the game. But more importantly, says Dr. Levine, the child laughs because he has mastered[3] an anxiety.

6   Adult laughter is more subtle,[4] but we also laugh at what we used to fear. The feeling of achievement, or lack of it, remains a crucial[5] factor. Giving a first dinner party is an anxious event for a new bride. Will the food be good? Will the guests get along? Will she be a good hostess? All goes well; the party is over. Now she laughs freely. Her pleasure from having proved her success is the foundation for her pleasure in recalling the evening's activities. She couldn't enjoy the second pleasure without

---

[1]**ogles:** stares at in an amorous manner
[2]**dowdy:** shabby
[3]**mastered:** learned to control
[4]**subtle:** not immediately obvious
[5]**crucial:** of decisive importance

the first, more important one—her mastery of anxiety.

7   Laughter is a social response triggered by cues. Scientists have not determined a brain center for laughter, and they are perplexed[6] by patients with certain types of brain damage who go into laughing fits for no apparent reason. The rest of us require company, and a reason to laugh.

8   When we find ourselves alone in a humorous situation, our usual response is to smile. Isn't it true that our highest compliment to a humorous book is to say that "it made me laugh out loud"? Of course, we do occasionally laugh alone; but when we do, we are, in a sense, socializing with ourselves. We laugh at a memory, or at a part of ourselves.

9   Practically every philosopher since Plato has written on how humor and laughter are related, but Sigmund Freud was the first to evolve a conclusive theory. Freud recognized that we all repress certain basic but socially "unacceptable" drives, such as sex and aggression. Jokes, not accidentally, are often based on either sex or aggression, or both. We find these jokes funny because they provide a sudden release of our normally suppressed drives. We are free to enjoy the forbidden, and the energy we normally use to inhibit these drives is discharged in laughter.

10   Another reason laughter is pleasurable is because of the physical sensations involved. Laughter is a series of minor facial and respiratory convulsions that stimulates our respiratory and circulatory systems. It activates the secretion of adrenalin and increases the blood flow to the head and brain. The total effect is one of euphoria.

11   Of course, we don't always need a joke to make us laugh. People who survive frightening situations, such as a fire or an emergency plane landing, frequently intersperse their story of the crisis with laughter. Part of the laughter expresses relief that everything is now all right. During a crisis, everyone mobilizes[7] energy to deal with the potential problem. If the danger is averted, we need to release that energy. Some people cry; others laugh.

12   Part of the integral[8] pleasure of a joke is getting the point. But if the sexual or aggressive element of the joke is too thinly disguised, as in "sick" humor, the joke will leave us feeling guilty instead of amused. We may laugh—but in embarrassment. According to Dr. Grotjahn, "The disguise must go far enough to avoid guilt," but "not so far that the thrill of aggression is lost."

13   Which brings us to why women may not have found the joke about the man watering his wife very funny—because they get the point only too well. Many psychiatrists agree that the reason women aren't amused by this kind of joke is that most sex jokes (a hefty[9] percentage of all jokes) employ women as their target. Women sometimes make poor joke tellers for the same reason; consciously or subconsciously, they express their resentment by "forgetting" the story.

14   When we are made the butt[10] of a joke, either on a personal or impersonal level, we are emotionally involved in it. Consequently, we won't be able to laugh (except as a pretense). While we are feeling, we cannot laugh. The two do not mix. French essayist Henri Bergson called laughter a "momentary anesthesia of the heart." We call it comic relief.

---

[6]**perplexed:** puzzled
[7]**mobilizes:** makes capable of movement
[8]**integral:** essential
[9]**hefty:** large
[10]**butt:** a person serving as the object of ridicule

15   Knowing that laughter blunts emotion, we can better understand why we sometimes laugh when nothing is funny. We laugh during moments of anxiety because we feel no mastery over the situation, claims Dr. Levine. He explains, "Very often compulsive laughter is a learned response. If we laugh, it expresses good feelings and the fact that we are able to cope. When we're in a situation in which we *can't* cope, we laugh to reassure ourselves that we *can!*"

16   How often have we laughed at a funeral or upon hearing bad news? We laugh to deny an unendurable reality until we are strong enough to accept it. Laughter also breaks our tension. However, we may also be laughing to express relief that the tragedy didn't happen to us. We laugh before giving a big party, before delivering a speech, or while getting a traffic ticket, to say, "This isn't bothering me. See? I'm laughing."

17   But if we sometimes laugh in sorrow, more often we laugh with joy. Laughter creates and strengthens our social bonds. And the ability to share a laugh has guided many marriages through hard periods of adjustment.

18   According to Dr. Levin, we can measure our adjustment to the world by our capacity to laugh. When we are secure about our abilities, we can poke fun at our foibles. If we can laugh through our anxieties, we will not be overpowered by them.

19   The ability to laugh starts early, but it takes a lifetime to perfect. Says Dr. Grotjahn, "When social relationships are mastered, when the individual has mastered... a peaceful relationship with himself, then he has ... the sense of humor." And then he can throw back his head and laugh.

After You Read

● Understanding Specialized Vocabulary

As you have seen in earlier units, every field of study possesses its own words and expressions. When we approach a reading that deals with a specific field, we need to familiarize ourselves with its language. This exercise will help to develop your vocabulary in the field of psychology.

DIRECTIONS: The first column is a list of words and expressions that have special meanings in the field of psychology. Find them in the text, and try to guess their meanings from the context. Note the ones that you are still unsure of. Then match each word or phrase with its synonym or meaning given in the second column (write the answer in the space provided), and check your answers by replacing the word with its definition in the context of the article.

1. schizophrenic psychosis   _____

2. mastery over an anxiety   _____

3. triggered by cues   _____

4. repress/inhibit   _____

5. drives   _____

6. aggression   _____

7. suppressed   _____

8. discharged   _____

9. secretion of adrenalin   _____

10. euphoria   _____

11. consciously   _____

12. subconsciously   _____

13. resentment   _____

14. compulsive   _____

a. overcoming nervousness or fear
b. in an aware manner
c. basic urges
d. released
e. set off by stimulae
f. hold back
g. hostile or angry behavior
h. feeling of well-being
i. bodily production of a hormone
j. in an unaware manner
k. uncontrollable
l. serious mental illness
m. angry indignation
n. kept from appearing

• Using Illustrative Examples in Cause/Effect Relationships

Throughout the article the author tells why people laugh and gives examples that illustrate these apparent reasons. By adding these examples, Janet Spencer has strengthened her argument and made it clearer. Her purpose of informing her audience and having them identify with the various interpretations of laughter is well served.

DIRECTIONS: The following is a list of examples that the author of "Why We Laugh" uses to develop the reasons for why people laugh. Match each of the examples with the reason it illustrates. You will need to refer to the reading to do this exercise. Write the reason in the space provided.

1. A child laughs when his father playfully tosses him in the air (after the first time).

   He has mastered an anxiety.

2. A bride laughs after successfully hosting her first dinner party.

   _____

3. We laugh at jokes about sex or aggression.

   _____

4. People who have survived a crisis laugh when telling about it later.

   _____

5. We might laugh on hearing bad news.

   _____

6. We might laugh while getting a traffic ticket.

   _____

Compare your answers with your classmates' answers, and compile a list of reasons why people laugh. You might add some reasons that Janet Spencer does not mention. Finally, go back to the freewriting you did before reading to reconsider the reason you gave for having laughed.

Becoming a Proficient Writer

Cohesion: Expressing Cause and Effect Relationships

In the preceding exercise you established reasons for people laughing in a variety of situations. The relationship between our laughter in these situations and the reasons we laugh is a **cause and effect relationship.** Our laughter is the effect or result. The causes of our laughter are the reasons that we laugh.

The English language has many ways of showing the cause and effect relationship between ideas. The following chart contains the most common expressions used to establish this relationship.

DIRECTIONS: In the preceding exercise, you were given an example (the effect) and asked to find a reason (the cause). Use expressions found in the following chart to combine the two ideas in items 2 through 6 in the preceding exercises.

Example: 1. A child laughs when his father playfully tosses him in the air (after the first time) *because* people laugh to express mastery over anxiety.

Expressions Used to Show Cause and Effect Relationships

	Introduces Cause	Introduces Effect	Grammatical Considerations*	Examples
Coordinating Conjunctions	for	so	Cause, so + effect.	I thought the joke was funny, so I laughed.
Subordinating Conjunctions	because, since		Because + cause, effect. *or* Effect because + cause.	Because the joke was funny, I laughed. I laughed because I thought the joke was funny.
Transitional Expressions		therefore, thus, consequently, as a result, for this reason	Cause. Therefore, effect. *or* Cause; therefore, effect.	I thought the joke was funny. Therefore, I laughed. I thought the joke was funny; therefore, I laughed.
Verbs (+ noun)	be caused by, result from	cause, result in	Effect be caused by cause. *or* Cause result in effect.	Laughter is caused by a number of psychological factors. A mastery of anxiety often results in laughter.
Phrases (+ noun)	because of, as a result of		Because of + cause, effect. *or* Effect because of + cause.	Because of his funny joke, we all laughed. We all laughed because of his funny joke.

*Pay attention to punctuation and capitalization shown here.

Generating Ideas

● Clustering

To help you to further explore the psychological implications of laughter, we introduce you to still another method for idea generation called **clustering.** Clustering is a kind of organized brainstorming. It leads you from a general idea to more specific aspects of that idea. By using clustering, you can either find topics you would like to write about or details you could use to develop an idea you already have. This technique is easy to use. Here are the steps you need to follow.

DIRECTIONS: Follow these steps to generate ideas about this topic.

1. Write the subject you are considering in the middle of a sheet of paper. In this case, "laughter."

2. Now brainstorm ideas you have about some aspect of laughter, for example, results of laughter. Draw lines coming from the subject in the center to each of the results of laughter you can think of. We've started a cluster with your classmates, try adding more ideas.

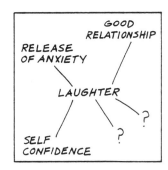

3. After you have exhausted these ideas, look over what you have written and choose one or more that interest you. From each of these, do another cluster which will introduce more specific ideas that develop that idea, for example, the benefits of self-confidence.

4. If you can draw more clusters from this subset, continue this process until you've run out of ideas. You might end up with several levels of clusters!

5. Look over what you have written and select the topics that apeal to you the most. These will be the subject of a freewriting.

Note: To see a full cluster, refer to unit 10, p. 246.

● Freewriting and Looping

Freewrite about two of the ideas in your cluster. Continue by making a loop for each of these freewritings.

Sharing Your Ideas

In small groups, talk about your freewritings. Then, using the list of reasons for laughing that you class compiled (p. 186), find examples to illustrate each reason. (Expand your list of reasons, if possible.)

LESSON 2

HOW TO BUILD
A HEALTHY RESPONSE
TO STRESS

About the Selection:

Our discussion of laughter presents a modern perspective on an age-old human response. Stress, another yet almost opposite human response, has actually been affected by changes in the modern world. Once people's basic survival response, stress would produce a burst of adrenalin, stimulating our ability to battle against life-threatening situations. Twentieth-century stress, on the other hand, has become a "raging tiger" threatening our mental and physical health. Today, modern science is combatting this hazard by first looking at its causes. In this excerpt from "Stress Management," authors Charlesworth and Nathan summarize the findings and resulting recommendations from an important study on the causes of stress.

The First Reading

Before You Read: Exploring Your Own Ideas

Think back over the past month. Have there been moments when you have felt stress? In the middle of a sheet of paper, write the word *stress*.

Now, make a cluster of the things that made you feel stress. Try to make the first level of your cluster more general. Then add levels to your cluster that are more specific.

As You Read: Looking for the Main Idea through Inferencing

Look for a relationship between the ideas you generated in your cluster and the causes of stress mentioned in the article.

HOW TO BUILD A HEALTHY RESPONSE TO STRESS

By Edward A. Charlesworth
and Ronald G. Nathan

Following is an excerpt from "Stress Management" (Atheneum, 1984) by Edward A. Charlesworth of the Baylor College of Medicine and Ronald G. Nathan of the Department of Psychiatry and Family Medicine at Louisiana State University Medical School in Shreveport.

1   It is said that about the only thing that we can count on in life, besides death and taxes, is change. Modern life presents us with more changes than ever before. We change everything rapidly: Where we live and work, our friends and even our spouses.

2   Change of any sort can be scary or exciting, and it usually triggers[1] our stress response.

3   Dr. Thomas Holmes and Dr. Richard Rahe at the University of Washington

School of Medicine have made major breakthroughs in our understanding of the effects of life changes on health and disease. Drs. Holmes and Rahe have measured the life changes that seem to precede illnesses.

4   From case histories of 5,000 patients, they gathered a long list of life events that seemed to precede major illnesses. They then asked about 400 people to compare the amount, intensity and length of time they need to adjust to each life event on the list.

5   Drs. Holmes, Rahe, and others, multiplied the number of times an event was experienced by the readjustment value given to the events and summed these products to find a life-change score.

6   Those who had a high life-change

[1]**triggers:** sets off

score were much more likely to contract an illness following the events. The illnesses ranged widely, from accidents to alcoholism, from cancer to psychiatric disorders, and from flu to the common cold.

[7]   To find your social readjustment rate, use the scale below. Take your time and try to include any event that is similar to the one given in the scale. When you are finished, total your life change units for the past year.

[8]   In general, a score of 150 to 300 is considered moderate,[2] while a score of more than 300 is considered high. High scores have been correlated with susceptibility[3] to illness and accidents in large group studies. But if you scored more than 300, it does not mean you are going to get sick or have an accident.

[9]   People seem to respond on an individual basis depending upon how much hassle each life event creates for a particular person. For example, people who have clear and meaningful goals or tend to be stimulus-seekers seem to be able to withstand more change.

[10]   Regardless of your score, you may find the following techniques helpful in managing stress.

[11]   The first step Dr. Holmes suggests is that we all become familiar with the life events and become aware of the amount of change they require.

[12]   Don't be fooled by the tendency to view positive changes such as marital reconciliation or gaining a new family member as free of stress. These also take a great deal of adaptive[4] energy.

[13]   An important part of stress-management training is to realize that some life crises are predictable. We all go through a series of stable periods alternating with transitional periods.

[14]   During stable periods, we make certain crucial choices and seek to attain particular goals and values. During transitional periods, we work toward terminating previous patterns and begin to work toward initiating new patterns.

[15]   One of the first major transition periods that adults go through begins at the end of adolescence. This transition may start around the age of 17 and last until about 22. During this transition, we begin to modify existing relationships with important individuals, groups and institutions.

[16]   Between the ages of 22 and 28 choices are made regarding occupation, relationships, values and life styles. As individuals begin to approach their late 20s, they may begin to question the commitments they have made previously.

[17]   About the age 30, a major transition period occurs. During this period, a person becomes more serious, more restrictive and more "for real." People feel a strong need to move forward and to produce the elements that they may feel are missing from their lives.

[18]   During the transition period, marital problems and divorce peak. It is often a time for changes in occupation or for settling down after transient jobs.

[19]   After going through this period of transition, a person reaches a settling-down point that may last from the age of about 32 until the ages of 39 or 40. During this period, the major tasks to accomplish include establishing a place in society and "making it" in a vocation.

[20]   The midlife transition, which occurs next, may last from 40 to 45. At this time, people may begin to question what they have done with their lives. They try to discover their real values.

[21]   According to one study of individuals going through the midlife transition, about

[2]**moderate:** average
[3]**susceptibility:** liability to be stricken with
[4]**adaptive:** able to become adjusted to a new situation

80% of the people experience very severe struggles within themselves and the external world.

22 It is important to realize as you learn how to manage stress that these life changes and crises are very normal parts of development.

23 Boredom is also a change stressor because the lack of change often brings on boredom. When we are not excited about what we are doing, we often become depressed, irritated and uptight. It is during times of boredom that we may wish to consider making some of the changes we can control on the Social Readjustment Rating Scale.

24 If your score on the Social Readjustment Rating Scale is less than 50, it might be healthy to take action to increase your change score. If you have a low score and you feel stressed, you could be experiencing boredom.

25 Most of us are striving for a happy and meaningful life. Balance is needed to achieve and maintain such a life. Balance means that you avoid building your life around one person or one thing.

26 Sigmund Freud considered work, play and love to be three major parts of life. Other psychotherapists have called these by other names, but most agree that they are important building blocks for a balanced life. If we ignore any one of them, we ask too much of the other two.

27 If you review the Social Readjustment Rating scale you will notice that a majority of the life events involve loved ones and life.

28 When things go wrong at work or we are unable to play because of illness, we experience a great deal of stress. Without a network of friends and family, we have no one with whom to share our troubles. Likewise, when things go our way, we have no one with whom to enjoy the pleasure. Loneliness is a major form of stress.

29 If, on the other hand, we do not know how to enjoy life and to maintain outside interests in hobbies, sports and the arts, we lose our ability to play, and we may put too much emphasis on work and love.

30 What if you are not interested in one or two of these factors? If so, it may be worthwhile to review your life situation and to pay particular attention to the factors you are ignoring to see if there is a conflict that needs your attention. Most people have very strong needs for work, play and love. Try to recognize and fulfill your needs in each of these areas.

THE SOCIAL READJUSTMENT RATING SCALE

Directions: Read each event and indicate in the space provided the number of times you have experienced the event in the last year. Multiply the number of times you experienced the event by the points next to it and total up the products.

LIFE EVENT	STRESS VALUE		NO. OF TIMES YOU EXPERIENCED THE EVENT LAST YEAR	YOUR TOTAL LIFE CHANGE SCORES
1. Death of spouse	100	X	_____	_____
2. Divorce	73	X	_____	_____
3. Marital separation from mate	65	X	_____	_____
4. Detention in jail or institution	63	X	_____	_____
5. Death of a close family member	63	X	_____	_____
6. Major personal injury or illness	53	X	_____	_____
7. Marriage	50	X	_____	_____

LIFE EVENT	STRESS VALUE	NO. OF TIMES YOU EXPERIENCED THE EVENT LAST YEAR	YOUR TOTAL LIFE CHANGE SCORES
8. Being fired from work	47	X	———— ————
9. Marital reconciliation with mate	45	X	———— ————
10. Retirement from work	45	X	———— ————
11. Major change in the health of a family member	44	X	———— ————
12. Pregnancy	40	X	———— ————
13. Sexual difficulties	39	X	———— ————
14. Gaining a new family member (e.g. through birth, adoption, oldster moving in, etc.)	39	X	———— ————
15. Major business readjustment (e.g. merger, reorganization, bankruptcy, etc.)	39	X	———— ————
16. Major change in financial state (e.g. a lot worse off or a lot better than usual)	38	X	———— ————
17. Death of a close friend	37	X	———— ————
18. Changing to a different line or work	36	X	———— ————
19. Major change in the number of arguments with spouse (e.g. either a lot more or less than usual regarding childbearing, personal habits, etc.)	35	X	———— ————
20. Taking on a mortgage greater than $10,000 (e.g. purchasing a home, business, etc.)	31	X	———— ————
21. Foreclosure on a mortgage or loan	30	X	———— ————
22. Major change in responsibilities at work (e.g. promotion, demotion, lateral transfer)	29	X	———— ————
23. Son or daughter leaving home (e.g. marriage, attending college, etc.)	29	X	———— ————
24. In-law troubles	29	X	———— ————
25. Outstanding personal achievement	28	X	———— ————
26. Wife beginning or ceasing work outside the home	26	X	———— ————
27. Beginning or ceasing formal schooling	26	X	———— ————
28. Major change in living conditions (e.g. building a new home, remodeling, deterioration of home or neighborhood)	25	X	———— ————
29. Revision of personal habits (e.g. dress, manners, associations, etc.)	24	X	———— ————
30. Troubles with the boss	23	X	———— ————
31. Major change in working hours or conditions	20	X	———— ————
32. Change in residence	20	X	———— ————
33. Change to a new school	20	X	———— ————
34. Major change in usual type and/or amount of recreation	19	X	———— ————
35. Major change in church activities (e.g. a lot more or a lot less than usual)	19	X	———— ————
36. Major change in social activities (e.g. clubs, dancing, movies, visiting, etc.)	18	X	———— ————
37. Taking on a mortgage or loan of less than $10,000 (e.g. purchasing a car, TV, freezer, etc.)	17	X	———— ————

LIFE EVENT	STRESS VALUE	NO. OF TIMES YOU EXPERIENCED THE EVENT LAST YEAR	YOUR TOTAL LIFE CHANGE SCORES
38. Major change in sleeping habits (e.g. a lot more or a lot less sleep or change in part of day when asleep)	16	X _____	_____
39. Major change in number of family get-togethers (e.g. a lot more or a lot less than usual)	15	X _____	_____
40. Major change in eating habits (e.g. a lot more or a lot less food intake, or very different meal hours or surroundings)	15	X _____	_____
41. Vacation	13	X _____	_____
42. Christmas	12	X _____	_____
43. Minor violation of the law (e.g. traffic tickets, jaywalking, disturbing the peace, etc.)	11	X _____	_____
GRAND TOTAL			_____

Reprinted with permission from *The Journal of Psychosomatic Research*, Vol. 11. T.H. Holmes and R.H. Rahe, "The Social Readjustment Rating Scale," Copyright 1967 Pergamon Press plc.

After You Read: Guessing Vocabulary from Context

DIRECTIONS: Use the context provided to guess the meaning of the italicized word. Write a definition or synonym of that word. Then refer back to the context in which the word is found in the article to see if your understanding of the word appears to be accurate.

1. The *breakthrough* made by the scientists permitted the next research team to make even further progress. (paragraph 3)

_____

2. To determine what events influenced her to move away from home, we must look at everything that happened to her in the year that *preceded* her decision. (paragraph 4)

_____

3. The old man had undergone a series of stressful experiences which probably lowered his resistance to illness, resulting, finally, in his *contracting* the serious disease. (paragraph 6)

_____

4. We now know that the way a person deals with stressful life events will greatly affect that person's *susceptibility* to becoming ill. Those who attempt to remain in control in a stressful situation tend to fall ill less frequently. (paragraph 8)

_____

5. Once back together, both the husband and wife were so relieved by their *marital reconciliation* that neither one realized that this change, too, was stress producing. (paragraph 12)

_____

6. Because the young student was unconsciously rejecting responsibilities, she failed to make a *commitment* to her studies, which resulted in poor results in her exams. (paragraph 16)

_____

The Second Reading

As You Read: Understanding the Author's Plan

Make a list of the causes of stress given in the article. Notice that there are only three major ideas given; the rest of the article is supporting information that the authors used to develop their main points.

After You Read

• Recognizing Supporting Evidence

DIRECTIONS: As a class or with a partner, decide on what the three main causes for stress are as stated in the article. Enter those ideas in the space provided. Then for each of the details listed, determine which cause they support. Write the letter of the corresponding cause in the space to the left of the detail.

MAIN IDEA—CAUSE

A. _____   B. _____   C. _____

SUPPORTING POINTS

_____ 1. We question commitment in our twenties.

_____ 2. We lack a network of friends.

_____ 3. We are not excited about what we are doing.

_____ 4. We gain a new family member.

_____ 5. We try to discover our real values.

_____ 6. We terminate previous patterns.

_____ 7. We are unable to play because of illness.

_____ 8. We lose our ability to play.

● Taking A Deeper Look: Understanding Cause and Effect Relationships

The relationship between the three causes we have just looked at and their result, stress, is clearly a cause and effect relationship. We can say, for example, that life changes, like a change in work, are the cause and stress is the effect. This is obvious. However, cause and effect relationships are not always as simple as this example appears. In fact, if we further consider this example, we will see how the resulting stress might not be caused by one isolated occurrence, like a change in work.

DIRECTIONS: You and a partner will "play detective" in discovering the relationship between the events in the life of a young man, which are listed chronologically here. Your job as, perhaps, the famous Sherlock Holmes is to use the events as clues to a mystery. To solve the mystery, you need to determine _why the young man has started drinking._ Use the article, "How to Build A Healthy Response to Stress," to analyze this case.

EVENTS:
- a. celebrates thirtieth birthday
- b. is promoted at work from a bus mechanic to a management position
- c. starts working overtime
- d. has a fight with wife
- e. feels stress
- f. starts drinking alcohol frequently

1. Is there one main cause?
2. Are there several causes?
3. Is there a series of causes?
4. Are the events related to each other?

When you have established the relationship between the events, compare the results of your investigation with the results of the other "detective teams" in your class.
    Note: Consider that all events are significant.

DO NOT READ BEYOND THIS POINT UNTIL ALL DETECTIVES HAVE SOLVED THE MYSTERY.
    GOOD LUCK, SHERLOCK HOLMES! GOOD LUCK, DR. WATSON!

● Analyzing Cause and Effect Relationships

Before comparing answers with your classmates, it is important to look at the question of **assumptions**. To solve this mystery, you had to *assume* that certain things were true. You guessed that certain of the clues were related. Depending on the assumptions made by the various detective teams, the mystery might have different solutions. Here are two possibilities:

If we assume that (1) the wife is unhappy about the husband's sudden increase in work hours, (2) their argument is about that subject (either directly or indirectly), (3) he feels stressed when they argue, and (4) he drinks when he is upset, then we can say that there is a **chain reaction.**

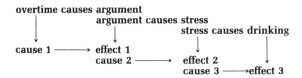

Each link of a chain reaction can be categorized. The cause closest to the effect is the **immediate cause.** As we have seen here, the immediate cause can be the result of an earlier cause or causes, called **proximate causes.** More distant, underlying causes are **remote causes.** If the husband's job change was a result of his going through a transition period, we could say that his age, 30, is a remote cause.

On the other hand, if we assume that (1) the husband is going through a stressful transition period, (2) the husband's job change was not a result of his transition period, (3) the overtime is not related to the promotion, (4) the husband is having difficulty adjusting to both the responsibility and the long hours at work, (5) the wife is delighted that her husband is getting more involved in his work (perhaps she is a career woman who works long hours, too), and (6) the argument is about something totally unrelated (consciously and unconsciously), then we can say that the causes of stress are all **contributing causes.**

Becoming a Proficient Writer

Guided Writing: Expressing Cause and Effect Relationships

Assume the role of Dr. Watson, the admiring friend of England's fictitious amateur detective, Sherlock Holmes. As always, you dutifully record the triumphs of Mr. Holmes. The solution to the mystery just solved by Holmes is so brilliant that you have decided to send a report to put to shame the London Metropolitan Police at Scotland Yard. Write this report, explaining the solution to the mystery. Don't forget to include the assumptions made. Carry on, Dr. Watson!

LESSON 3

COMPOSING ON YOUR OWN

The First Draft

Choosing a Topic and Generating Ideas

DIRECTIONS: After choosing one of the following topics, use the idea-generating techniques that you find the most productive to begin the process. Then write the first draft.

A. Using what you have learned from the article on stress and your understanding of the complexity of most cause and effect relationships, write an essay in which you discuss the major causes of stress in your life and how these causes are related to one another. *Suggestion:* Fill out the social readjustment rating scale found in lesson 2. Then brainstorm a list of things that seem to make you feel stress.

B. The following poem by Charles Bukowski illustrates the belief that it is the everyday annoyances of life and not major life changes that are responsible for stress.

> *...It's not the large things that*
> *send a man to the*
> *madhouse... no, it's the*
>   *continuing series of*
> *small tragedies*
> *that send a man to the madhouse*
>   *. . .*
> *not the death of his love*
> *but a shoelace that snaps*
> *with no time left...*

"the shoelace," copyright © 1972 by Charles Bukowski. Reprinted from *Mockingbird Wish Me Luck* with permission of Black Sparrow Press.

Take a stand on this issue and argue your point in a well-developed essay. (For the second draft you might want to refer back to the comparison-contrast essay organization discussed in unit 7.)

C. In the article on stress, the authors mention that some people tend to be able to withstand more stress than others. In the article on laughter, we learned that "if we can laugh at our anxieties, we will not be overpowered by them." Combine these two ideas in an essay in which you show the relationship between laughter and our ability to cope with stress. Use specific examples taken from your own life and/or the lives of people you know.

Consider the content aspects of the first draft and revise.

The Second Draft

Checking Cause and Effect for Logical Fallacies

Once you have revised your paper for content, you can begin to consider the organization and logic aspects of it. Essays involving cause and effect should be checked at this point for a common problem that occurs in this type of writing, **logical fallacies** or errors in reasoning. Because of the nature of the cause-effect relationship, these errors in reasoning often take one of several forms. They are as follows:

1. **Oversimplification:** This occurs when we assume that a complex issue has simply one cause or simple causes. We do not consider contributing or chain reaction causes.

    Example: The thirty-year-old started drinking heavily because he had a fight with his wife.

2. **Lack of evidence:** We sometimes make statements that we do not support. We need to use our experiences and education to support our analysis, to prove our point.

    Example: The thirty-year-old's stress is obviously due to his age. (doesn't explain the statistics about the transition stage he is probably going through)

3. **Post hoc:** We incorrectly assume that a time relationship is a cause-effect relationship.

   Example: The couple had a fight because he was working late. (assumes that the wife is unhappy about the overtime)

Check your essay for these types of logical fallacies. Once you have made any necessary changes, you are ready to peeredit.

Peerediting, Revising, and Rewriting

By this point of the text, you have had many experiences editing the papers of your classmates. Up until now, we have provided you with guidelines to use during these sessions. For this writing assignment, we put the responsibility into your hands. Choose a classmate whom you have worked with before. Together, come up with a list of peerediting guidelines that covers all of the important aspects of a well-written essay that you have considered before, and then include questions that cover the new material you have learned in this unit. Once you have agreed on the guidelines, use them to peeredit. Then revise/rewrite your paper.

Proofreading

In lesson 1 you worked with sentence combining. Naturally, being a cause-effect essay, your paper will include some of the expressions that were proposed in the chart in lesson 1 on page 187. Besides proofreading for recurring grammatical problems, check for sentence-combining problems. Here are some questions that you might use as guidelines to check your sentence-combining proficiency.

1. Are all sentences complete?
2. Was I careful not to use a subordinator *and* a coordinator to combine two clauses?

   Example: Since he worked overtime,
              so his wife and he had a quarrel.

3. Did I use the proper punctuation between clauses?

   Example: He worked late,
              therefore, they had a quarrel.

4. Do the expressions I used to combine ideas really express the true relationship between those ideas?

   Example: He worked late
              so that they had a quarrel.

5. Did I use a variety of expressions? How many times did I use *and* to combine two clauses?

6. Do I meaningfully employ a variety of sentences? (simple, compound, complex)

Sharing Your Writing

Several students in the class will read their essays, or the teacher will read them. These essays will present different views on the same subject. Use the evidence presented in the essays to have an open, informal class debate on the different points of view. Be sure to take a stand on the issue before the debate begins. You might want to write down a simple statement expressing your opinion before the debate and then do the same after the debate to see if the class discussion swayed your opinion. The activity should culminate in a vote for the point of view that had the most convincing evidence.

Keeping a Journal

1. Describe a moment in your life that was particularly stressful but that you were able to cope with. Analyze what you did or what helped you to overcome this difficult moment. Did you learn an important lesson from the experience?
2. Many psychologists believe that there is a positive and necessary kind of stress called *eustress*. Eustress gets your adrenalin going, as does *distress* (bad stress), but it makes people feel good and can stimulate productive energy. Describe instances of eustress in your life, and explain how they have been productive experiences.
3. Describe the funniest moment in your life, and analyze why it was so funny. (Try not to laugh too hard while you're writing!)

UNIT NINE

IN DELICATE BALANCE: ECOLOGY

LESSON 1

AS RARE PANDAS LUMBER TOWARD EXTINCTION

Marsha L. Botsford

Considering the Topic

Before we introduce the first reading selection for this unit, take a few moments to consider the topic, the giant panda, in order to gather your own thoughts and feelings about it.

DIRECTIONS: Look at the picture of the giant panda on the previous page. What do you think of when you see this animal? What feelings, images, or concerns does it evoke? Use the cluster technique that you learned in unit 8 to help you collect your thoughts.

1. Create a cluster around the word *panda.*
2. Choose one of the words you have written which you would like to explore further. As you did in unit 8, develop a second cluster around this word. If possible, continue this branching-out process with a third or even fourth cluster until you've exhausted your ideas.
3. Choose one branch of the cluster and write the topic of that branch at the top of a new sheet of paper. (An example might be "The Panda: A Beautiful Animal.") Based on the ideas generated in your cluster, freewrite for ten minutes on this topic.

Sharing Your Ideas

In small groups or together as a class, discuss briefly the ideas which emerged from your clustering exercise. Did you have the same reaction to the picture as your classmates did? What different ideas or issues did you write about? Share your knowledge as well as your images of the rare and popular animal.

About the Selection:

The giant panda of China provides a striking contrast to today's world. With its slow, lumbering movements, it appears unimpressed with the speed and urgency of modern society. Unable, however, to escape the effects of human society, it hides reclusively from humans and their frenzied activity. Today the life of the giant panda of China is greatly threatened. As the panda's territory has grown smaller due to agricultural and industrial development, so have its numbers. This beautiful creature now faces the threat of extinction. The following article taken from *U.S. News & World Report* describes the greatest threat to the panda and the tremendous international efforts to overcome it.

Before You Read: Guessing Vocabulary from Context

DIRECTIONS: Use the contexts given to guess the meaning of the indicated words. Write your guess and the clues you used in the space provided. Your understanding of these words will help you with the reading selection.

1. Scan the passage entitled "About the Selection" to find the four words listed here. Use the context to guess their meaning.

   a. *lumbering:* _____

      clues: _____

   b. *reclusively/reclusive:* _____

      clues: _____

   c. *rare:* _____

      clues: _____

   d. *extinction:* _____

      clues: _____

2. "The greatest *peril* to the panda is man himself... For the moment, however, the threat is not of man's making, but of nature's."

      peril: _____

      clues: _____

3. "The favorite food of the panda, arrow bamboo, has begun a once-in-decades flowering cycle in which the *edible* adult shoots wither (dry up) and then die. It will be a decade (ten years) before new plants spawned by this die-off *mature*."

   a. *edible:* _____
      clue: Use the parts of the word. You know the meaning of the suffix *-ible*. The stem *ed-* means "to eat."

   b. *mature:* _____

      clues: _____

4. "Many of the pandas that survive have been driven from their normal territory to *forage* for food.

      forage: _____

      clues: _____

As You Read: Looking for the Main Ideas

As you read, consider the following questions.

1.   What event in nature is threatening the giant panda?
2.   Have the efforts to save the panda been successful? In what ways?
3.   What have been the failures in this effort?
4.   What major problem does the relief program have?
5.   What is the greatest long-term danger to the panda?

AS RARE PANDAS LUMBER TOWER TOWARD EXTINCTION
By Walter A. Taylor

Under Pressure from Man and Nature, the Reclusive Animal Is Imperiled by Starvation and Attack from the World Outside

WOLONG PANDA PRESERVE, China

1   Here in the misty mountains and unspoiled magnificence of South China's largest wilderness area, man is battling to save the rare giant panda from extinction.

2   As few as 100 of the lumbering, black-and-white animals—one tenth of those left in the wild—remain here, pushed into the remote areas of the rugged peaks and scenic valleys.

3   The greatest peril to the panda is man himself and his tightening encirclement of this and other final refuges.[1]

4   For the moment, however, the threat is not of man's making, but of nature's. The favorite food of the panda, arrow bamboo, has begun a once-in-decades[2] flowering cycle in which edible adult shoots wither and then die. It will be a decade before new plants spawned by the die-off mature.

5   As the process spreads throughout the region, some pandas are starving to death. In the three Chinese provinces in which pandas can still be found (Sichuan, Gansu and Shanxi), at least 20 have died since last September, when Chinese and foreign naturalists first noticed the start of bamboo flowering.

6   Many of those that survive have been driven from their normal territories to forage for food. Mating[3] cycles have been dis-

[1]**refuges:** safe areas
[2]**decade:** ten years
[3]**mating cycle:** reproduction cycle

rupted. Some have begun eating twigs, tree leaves, and grass, a diet that lacks adequate nutrition and leaves them weak, vulnerable[4] to illness, and prone to falls from trees and cliffs.

7   Wildlife authorities in the Sichuan provincial capital of Chengdu warn that 70 to 90 percent of the arrow bamboo is withering in some areas, so the worst may be yet to come. In 1975–76, during another bamboo famine, 138 pandas—10 percent of the world panda population at that time— starved to death.

8   Yet there remains hope that another such disaster still can be avoided.

9 THE FAILURES. With the Switzerland-based World Wildlife Fund (WWF), China is making a concerted and dedicated effort to save the endangered animals. The results, officials here in Chengdu indicate, are mixed but encouraging.

10   A clear disappointment is the failure to breed[5] pandas in captivity,[6] necessary if their decreasing numbers are to be replaced. Natural and artificial techniques have been tried unsuccessfully at the modern research facilities run by the Sichuan Ministry of Forestry and the WWF.

11   Another failure has been the incapability to find a natural, readily available food to replace the arrow bamboo.

12 THE SUCCESSES. Despite these failures, success has come on two fronts. One achievement has been the physical rescue effort. While it cannot be certain that more pandas have not died in the inaccessible regions of Wolong and other preserves, the last reported deaths were in April, when four animals died.

13   Some pandas have been kept alive by salting[7] the rugged mountains with tons of cooked meat, which pandas will eat as a substitute for bamboo, and by the planting of new bamboo in isolated areas.

14   Animals in some Sichuan areas have been rescued by local peasants and given

---

[4]**vulnerable:** capable of being hurt; open to illness or attack
[5]**breed:** to reproduce; to cause an animal to bear offspring
[6]**in captivity:** confined by humans; not in the wild
[7]**salting:** to place into; to spread (the mountains) with (meat)

emergency treatment by veterinarians[8] of the Chinese Army and the Chengdu Zoo. In one recent case, a group of farmers discovered an injured panda, one that had tumbled from a high cliff, and carried it for 19 hours to a rescue center.

15   A second achievement is a massive fund-raising effort. Publicity about the pandas' plight has resulted in a new $100,000 emergency allocation by the WWF and independent fund drives both in China and abroad. It's been reported that funds from concerned Chinese have been rolling in at the equivalent of $3,000 per day.

16 PROBLEMS. In spite of this support, there have been conflicts in the panda relief program. One important problem is the difficulty Peking is having balancing the recommendations of environmentalists with China's ambitious goal of agricultural and industrial modernization.

17   Wolong is but one example of this difficulty. This 494,000-acre preserve was declared a protected area in 1975. Yet 1,800 people, mostly Tibetans, still live in the preserve, logging trucks still rumble down the narrow mountain roads, and

blasting work still goes on at the site of a new 160,000-kilowatt hydroelectric plant just six miles away.

18 DAMAGE "UNAVOIDABLE." One official of the Sichuan Forestry says that he and other naturalists opposed construction of the electric plant because ecological damage to the preserve would be "unavoidable."

19   According to the experts, such human activity prevents the normally reclusive pandas from moving to lower elevations of the preserve, where they could find alternative types of bamboo to eat.

20   Officials say there is a plan to move all people from Wolong once relocation funds become available. But that evacuation will take up to three years.

21   By the same token, the main road through the preserve is to be closed to truck traffic, but not until an alternative route can be constructed, another project that could take years.

22   This all means that the pandas' fight for survival will not be an easy one, even with the concerted effort of man. For in the end, even if they can survive the dangers of the wild, they must still contend with man himself.

[8]**veterinarians:** animal doctors

After You Read: Comprehending the General Meaning and Scanning

DIRECTIONS: Work alone and then with a partner. Don't refer to the article before answering the questions.

1. Look back at the main idea questions preceding the reading selection.
2. Without looking back at the article, jot down your answers to these questions.
3. After you have finished, compare your answers with those of a classmate. Refer to the article for information when your answers differ.
4. Then scan the article to find the answers to the following detailed questions.
   a. How many pandas are left in the wild today?

b. What percentage of the arrow bamboo was withering at the time of this article?

c. How many pandas died in the 1975–76 famine? Was this a significant number?

d. What is the name of the Switzerland-based organization funding the panda research project in Wolong? How much money was given to this project?

e. What three indications does the article give of harmful human activity in the Wolong preserve? Why is this activity damaging to the panda? How long will it take for this activity to be stopped?

Becoming a Proficient Writer

Generating Ideas: Using Your New Knowledge

In the reading selection and the preceding exercises, you probably acquired some knowledge about this creature which you did not have before. Perhaps you gained deeper insight into a problem of which you were already aware. At this time, it might be interesting to see which ideas from the article you have incorporated into your developing understanding of this issue.

DIRECTIONS: Follow these steps to expand your ideas about pandas.

1. Again take out a sheet of paper to create a cluster. This time, in the center of the paper write *panda: endangered*. Now develop a cluster around this new, more focused phrase. Don't refer back to the article. Rely on the ideas that come into your mind, either from the article or from your own experience and perspective.

2. After you have finished your cluster, choose one aspect to develop further in a second cluster and then in a freewriting.

3. Look over your cluster and freewriting. Can you detect any influence the article may have had on your thinking about this issue? Compare your ideas with those of your classmates. Did they respond to the same aspect of the problem as you did or to something different? Why do you think that two people reading the same article might focus in on different aspects of that article? Does this tell you anything about the reading process? The writing process?

LESSON 2

ECOSYSTEMS IN AND OUT OF BALANCE

About the Selection:

In the first lesson of this unit, you saw how the giant panda's changing environment has affected the life (and life expectancy) of this beautiful animal. The panda's situation, of course, is not unique. We all depend on our environment for survival. In fact, this dependency is so complex and so great that the study of it has developed from a minor branch of biology into a sophisticated science called environmental science, or *ecology.* This field of study focuses on the interrelationships of living organisms with each other and with their total environment. It studies *ecosystems,* which are groups of living things interacting together in their environment and, thereby, surviving. The following reading selection has been adapted from an introductory ecology textbook, *Environmental Science: The Way the World Works,* written by Dr. Bernard J. Nebel for American college students. "Ecosystems In and Out of Balance" is a condensed version of the second chapter of this text, which discusses the issue of ecosystem change.

The First Reading

Before You Read: Previewing a Textbook Chapter

Reading a textbook is somewhat different from most other kinds of reading. When you read a textbook, you generally need to comprehend the material more thoroughly and in more detail than when you read for pleasure or for general information only. Often you are trying to learn material and accompanying vocabulary that is entirely new and unfamiliar to you. To help yourself understand the reading and cope with new words and concepts, **preview** the chapter before you actually begin reading it. Previewing the chapter will give you a general picture of what the author is trying to accomplish and what information he or she sees as important. This knowledge will help you to comprehend the relationships between the ideas in the chapter and to learn the material more easily.

There are four main steps to previewing a chapter:

1. *Read the title and introduction to the chapter.* The title will give you the general topic, and the introduction (if there is one) will often provide you with a summary of what to expect in the chapter; for example, what questions the author seeks to answer or what issues he or she will address.

> DIRECTIONS: Read the introduction to the passage, "Ecosystems: Stable and Changing," and then answer the following questions.

a. What is the purpose of paragraph 1? _____

_____

What important information does it include? _____

_____

b. Underline the key question raised in paragraph 2. Note that this question presents a focus for the entire chapter.

c. What is the relationship between balance and change discussed in paragraph 3? _____

_____

d. Based on the title and the introduction, write a sentence describing what you expect the chapter to be about. _____

_____

2. *Read the questions at the end of the chapter* (if there are any). This will give you an idea of what ideas the author of the text thinks are important. Try to answer as many of the questions as you can before you read the chapter. This will make you think about the questions more as you preview and then read the chapter.

DIRECTIONS: This text does not have questions at the end of the chapters, so for the purposes of this exercise, read and try to answer the comprehension questions on page 220 of this unit.

3. *Skim through the chapter* to identify the main ideas and direction of the unit. To skim, read quickly over the subtitles in boldface print, the first paragraph of each main section, and the first sentence or two of each paragraph. Also note the pictures, charts, maps, or other graphics. Read the captions and try to paraphrase the main idea of each such illustration, as these are often important clues as to the author's intent in that section or chapter.

DIRECTIONS: Skim through the reading selection following the foregoing procedure.

4. *Try again to answer the questions at the end of the chapter.* You will probably be able to answer a few of them after having skimmed the chapter. Don't be concerned about those you can't answer. This second reading of the questions will help you to focus your attention on the points emphasized by the author.

DIRECTIONS: Follow step 4 for this reading selection by turning once again to the comprehension questions on page 220.

Now you are ready to read the chapter.

As You Read: Reading with a Purpose

1. Look for the answers to the questions you previewed as you try to get a better understanding of the main points of the chapter.
2. Like most textbooks, this text introduces new vocabulary which has specialized meanings in the field studied (ecology). It is important to pay attention to this technical vocabulary, as it will be used throughout the course of study. Underline technical words or expressions and then make a list of them and their definitions after you read. This will help you study the material later.
3. Also underline lightly (in pencil) other words or expressions which are new to you and whose meaning you do not know. Don't interrupt your first reading of the chapter to look up these words unless they are absolutely necessary for your understanding of a particular section. There will be ample time afterward to think about and look up these words if desired.

ECOSYSTEMS IN AND OUT OF BALANCE
by Bernard J. Nebel

Ecosystems: Stable and Changing

1   In the previous chapter we saw that ecosystems have a structure consisting of *producers* (green plants which use light energy to produce living matter from non-living matter in the environment), *consumers* (all the animals which feed directly or indirectly on the green plants), and *decomposers* (bacteria and fungi that change the dead organic material back into simpler raw materials which can then again be used by the producers. This structure, which is necessary to maintain the flow of energy and nutrients through the system, consists of the interactions between hundreds or even thousands of different kinds of plants, animals, and microbes which grow, reproduce and die in a never-ending cycle.

2   At this point, we might ask ourselves,

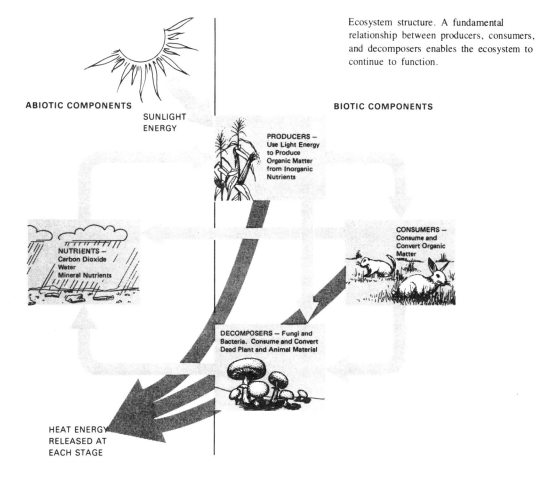

Ecosystem structure. A fundamental relationship between producers, consumers, and decomposers enables the ecosystem to continue to function.

ABIOTIC COMPONENTS

SUNLIGHT ENERGY

BIOTIC COMPONENTS

PRODUCERS — Use Light Energy to Produce Organic Matter from Inorganic Nutrients

NUTRIENTS — Carbon Dioxide Water Mineral Nutrients

CONSUMERS — Consume and Convert Organic Matter

DECOMPOSERS — Fungi and Bacteria, Consume and Convert Dead Plant and Animal Material

HEAT ENERGY RELEASED AT EACH STAGE

since ecosystems consist of the interactions between reproducing populations, what prevents one species (kind) of organism from reproducing in such numbers that it overcomes and eliminates other species? In other words, what are the factors that maintain the structure, or *balance,* of that ecosystem?

3   To answer that question we must first recognize that the idea of ecosystem balance is relative. In fact, ecosystems are always changing and adjusting. At some times certain species may increase in population; at other times they may decrease and be replaced by other species. In some cases the changes may be relatively fast, occurring over a period of only a few years. In other cases, changes may be very slow, occurring over many thousands or even millions of years. The relative degree of balance is the main factor in determining the rate of change. A well-balanced system will change very slowly, perhaps unnoticeably, in the course of direct human experience. An unbalanced system changes more or less rapidly; the greater the imbalance, the more rapid the change. It follows that if a change is made in one or more of the factors that affect balance, the ecosystem itself will also change.

Biotic Potential And Environmental Resistance

4   One way of viewing ecosystem change and balance is in terms of the two factors: *biotic potential* and *environmental resistance.*

5   The *biotic potential* of a species is its capacity for reproducing itself; in a general sense it is the combination of all the factors that permit its kind to become more numer-

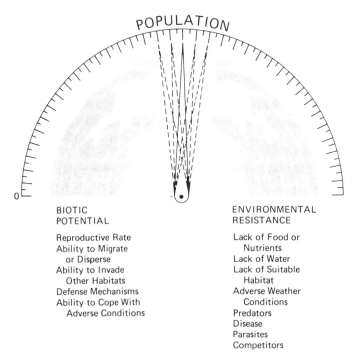

Population is a balance between factors that increase numbers and factors that decrease numbers.

ous. Birth rate is an obvious factor, but it is only one. The ability of animals to migrate or of seeds to disperse to similar habitats in other locations, the ability to adapt to and invade other habitats, defense mechanisms such as quills, thorns or bad smell, and the ability to avoid or survive difficult environmental conditions are equally important. Given favorable conditions, every species has a biotic potential to increase its population. For example, a pair of frogs has the biotic potential to produce several hundred offspring in one season and each offspring in turn could potentially produce several hundred more.

6   The fact that populations in nature generally do not "explode" in numbers is not due to limits in biotic potential, but to a second factor, *environmental resistance*. The environmental resistance facing each species is the combination of all the factors that limit the survival of its members. These factors are similar for both plants and animals. They include lack of food or nutrients, lack of water, lack of suitable habitat, harmful weather conditions, predators, diseases, parasites, and other organisms that are competing for the same habitat. Thus, there is a relationship between biotic potential and environmental resistance. If the environmental resistance for a species is less than its biotic potential, its numbers will increase; if the environmental resistance is greater than biotic potential, then its numbers will decrease. In a stable ecosystem, the biotic potential of each species is evenly balanced by environmental resistance.

Humankind And Ecosystem Balance

7   Now let's look at ourselves as a species in relation to ecosystem balance.

8   Modern scientists believe that humankind, like other animals, evolved through millions of years of changes and adaptations to the environment and that our most direct evolutionary ancestor was probably an earlier species of the primate (monkey, ape) group. Despite this similarity with other creatures, however, the evolution of humankind differs from that of other species in one important and unique way.

9   In other species evolution has led to *specialization*, both in the species abilities and in its place within the environmental structure. For example, the giraffe is marvelously adapted to grazing on treetops but, as such, it is also specialized and thus restricted to grazing on trees and shrubs. Only with great difficulty can it bend down to graze on the ground. Similarly, the anteater is extremely well adapted to eating ants but is incapable of catching or eating other prey. The same is true for countless other species.

10   For humankind the reverse is true. Our evolution had led to a very *generalized* capability. Our highly developed intelligence and ability to make and handle tools mean that we can do virtually anything. Rather than evolving into a specialized role in balance with natural enemies, competitive species and environmental factors, humans evolved in such a way that we are capable of moving into every environment on Earth and even into space. No natural predator or competitor offers significant resistance, and other natural enemies such as disease have been substantially controlled.

11   Said another way, we see in humankind a tremendous imbalance between biotic potential and environmental resistance. The result is the rapidly increasing world population, frequently referred to as the *population explosion*. Further, to support our growing population, natural ecosystems are being increasingly displaced by human habitations, agriculture, and other human-supporting activities.

What Does This Imbalance Mean for the Future?

[12]   From the viewpoint of evolutionary history, the spreading of human beings over the Earth can be looked at as a natural process, the latest of many waves of change that have occurred since the earliest beginnings of life on this planet. In our position as humans, however, we would like to see this latest wave (ourselves) as permanent or at least very long lasting. Unfortunately, there is nothing in ecological or evolutionary theory to support the view that humans will be the last or even a long-lasting "wave." In fact, there are many indications that the human wave, at least that of humans in a technological society, may be relatively short lived. Why is this so?

[13]   First the rate and degree of many changes being brought about by humans are extreme. Previous evolutionary changes have occurred over the course of many millions of years. Thus the slow processes of readaptation and development of new species more or less balanced extinctions, and ecosystems remained in relative balance throughout the course of change. In contrast, the significant changes brought about by humans have occurred in only the last 200 years. Before that time, lack of technological capability forced humans to live in relative ecological balance. Now, of course, this is no longer true. Moreover, the rate and degree of change continues to increase as jungles, forests and grasslands are converted to agricultural fields, cities and parking lots.

[14]   The result is that extinctions are occurring at a distressingly fast rate, a rate which is more than likely to increase in the future. Furthermore, the rapidity of the changes we are causing leaves no time for the development of new species to fill the places left vacant, and relatively few species have been able to adapt to new roles within the human environment. In short, changes in the biosphere are occurring so rapidly that we have no way of accurately predicting the outcome. Many ecologists are concerned that the basic balances within the biosphere will be so altered that all life on earth, including human life, will be disrupted.

[15]   Second, there is danger in the simplicity of the human ecosystem. Based as it is on relatively few species of agricultural crops and animals, the human ecosystem is inherently unstable. Agricultural production is only tenuously balanced by the massive use of powerful chemicals to control pests, and these chemicals are causing ecological upsets that frequently make pest problems even worse. Also, plant scientists warn that an outbreak of crop disease for which we do not have a cure could wipe out a significant portion of the world food supply in one season. A stable human ecosystem will require and depend upon balanced relationships with numerous other organisms in the biosphere. The importance of preserving other organisms and ecosystems should be seen in this light.

[16]   Third, there are many indications that present human expansion is resulting in *overgrazing* of vast areas of the Earth's surface. Overgrazing occurs when plant-eating populations expand to the point when they eat the vegetation faster than it can reproduce and, consequently, destroy it. Overgrazing of livestock around the world is converting millions of hectares of rangeland into worthless desert. In a region south of the Sahara, this has already led to massive starvation affecting both livestock and the people dependent on it.

[17]   Also, growth and maintenance of our technological society is based on increasing use of oil and natural gas, which clearly are

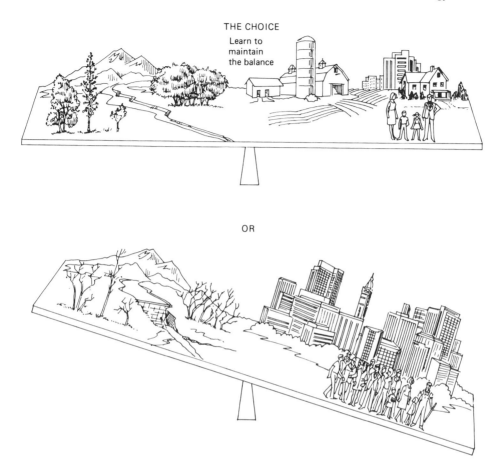

limited, nonrenewable resources. This is overgrazing in a figurative sense, but if carried to the end point, the results will be just as fatal.

18   In conclusion, there is no way that the human species can avoid facing the ultimate checks and balances that apply to other species and ecosystems. Ignoring this reality can only lead to disaster. Fortunately, however, ecological realities need not be ignored. We as humans do have the unique evolutionary traits of exceptional intelligence and technological capability. We have the potential to use these traits to make adjustments in our societies and lifestyles to live within ecological limits and in balance with the rest of the biosphere. It is largely a matter of choice whether we as individuals and as a society wish to continue on the path of overgrazing and increasing ecological instability until the system crumbles or whether we wish to establish our own limits and make the necessary changes toward balancing the human ecosystem with the rest of the biosphere.

Bernard J. Nebel from *Environmental Science: The Way the World Works*, first edition, Prentice Hall, Inc., 1981. Reprinted by permission.

After You Read

• Comprehending the Basic Meaning

DIRECTIONS: For questions 1 through 8, circle T if the statement is true; circle F if the statement is false. Answer questions 9 and 10 by providing short statements or phrases about the information requested. Try to answer the questions without looking back at the article; then scan the article to check your answers.

T F 1. The structure of an ecosystem is made up of producers and consumers, which interact with each other and with their environment.

T F 2. A balanced ecosystem is one which is stable and unchanging.

T F 3. The more unbalanced an ecosystem is, the more rapidly it will change.

T F 4. Biotic potential is the main factor determining the balance of an ecosystem.

T F 5. A species' birth rate is one part of its biotic potential.

T F 6. If the environmental resistance facing a species is higher than its biotic potential, then its numbers will increase.

T F 7. A rapid increase or decrease in the population of a single species could result in major changes in the ecosystem as a whole.

T F 8. Evolution has led to greater specialization in humans than in other animals, and this specialization has resulted in ecosystem imbalance.

9. What three indications are given that the ecological imbalance caused by humans may lead to ultimate disaster for humankind and for the world?

_____

_____

_____

10. Does the author believe that the situation for humankind is hopeless?

_____ Why or why not? _____

• Learning Technical Vocabulary

In your first reading of this chapter, you should have highlighted the following technical vocabulary. Most of these words are defined for you in the chapter; a few others you'll have to look up in the dictionary. Because it is important for you to learn the vocabulary used in any field you are studying, you will need to devise a technique for recording and studying these words. One method for doing this is to make a list of new words to be learned along with their definitions. It is often helpful to group these words into logical categories, as remembering the relationships between them will also help you to remember their meanings and significance.

DIRECTIONS: Where appropriate, the following technical terms are divided into categories (indicated by brackets). In the space to the left of each group, enter a logical title for that category. In the space to the right of each word, write the definition of the word given in the text.

$\Bigg\{$ producers: _____

consumers: _____

decomposers: _____

$\Big\{$ ecosystem: _____

ecosystem balance: _____

biotic potential: _____

environmental resistance: _____

overgrazing: _____

DIRECTIONS: The following are common terms with specific meanings in the context of this reading. Choose and underline the appropriate definition from the dictionary excerpt printed to the right of each word.*

specialization/specialize: spe·cial·i·za·tion (spĕsh′e-le-zā′shen) n. The action of specializing or the process of becoming specialized.
spe·cial·ize (spĕsh′e-līz′) v. **-ized, -izing, -izes.** —intr. 1. To train or employ oneself in a special study or activity. 2. *Biology.* To develop so as to become adapted to a specific environment or function. —tr. 1. To make specific mention of; particularize; specify. 2. To give a particular character or function to. 3. *Biology.* To adapt by specialization. 4. To specify the payee in endorsing (a check).

generalized capability: gen·er·al·ize (jĕn′er-e-līz′) v. **-ized, -izing, -izes.** —tr. 1. a. To reduce to a general form, class, or law. b. To render indefinite or unspecific. 2. a. To infer from many particulars. b. To draw inferences or a general conclusion from. 3. a. To make generally or universally applicable. b. To popularize. —intr. 1. a. To form a concept inductively. b. To form general notions or conclusions. 2. To speak or think in generalities; speak vaguely. 3. *Medicine.* To spread through the body. Said of a usually localized disease.

• Guessing Vocabulary from Context

DIRECTIONS: Follow these steps to address unfamiliar vocabulary words.

1. Scan the selection for the unfamiliar words you underlined.
2. Using the context, make a guess as to the word's meaning. You may want to jot down your guess in the margin of your text.
3. If the meaning of a particular term is unclear from the context and if this meaning is necessary to your comprehension of that section of the text, you'll need to use your dictionary. However, do not spend time looking up words unnecessarily. If a general understanding of the word is sufficient, spend your time working on more important concepts and information.
4. There may be some words that you will want to study and learn to use in the future. In this case, you might develop a list of important words and additional technical terms to add to the ones you just defined. You can then study these words and their definitions periodically until you have learned them.

The Second Reading

As You Read: Underlining and Marginal Glossing

Once you have read through a textbook selection once, you are ready for a more in-depth look at the material. Underlining key words as you read and jotting brief marginal notes will help you to focus on important points when you study the material later. Following is one example of how the first paragraph of this selection might be underlined and glossed. Note that this underlining is done during the *second* reading of the text, after you already have a general idea of the author's main points. Note also that only key words and phrases are underlined—*not* whole sentences.

In the previous chapter we saw that ecosystems have a structure consisting of producers (green plants which use light energy to produce living matter from non-living matter in the environment), consumers (all the animals which feed directly and indirectly on the green plants), and decomposers (bacteria and fungi which change the dead organic material back into simpler raw materials which can then again be used by the producers.) This structure, which is necessary to maintain the flow of energy and nutrients through the system, consists of the interactions between hundreds or even thousands of different kinds of plants, animals, and microbes which grow, reproduce, and die in a never-ending cycle.

Margin notes:

ecosystem =
producers (green plants)
+
consumers (animals)
+
decomposers
(bacteria +
fungi)

structure of
interactions →
cycle → flow
of energy and
nutrients

DIRECTIONS: As you read this selection for the second time, underline key words and phrases and write any marginal notes that seem appropriate. Read over the following study and discussion questions to get an idea of the kind of information you should be looking for.

After You Read: Answering Questions for Study and Discussion

It is often helpful to analyze a textbook reading section-by-section to get a more thorough understanding of the material covered. For this reason, the following study and discussion questions have been arranged by section and paragraph.

DIRECTIONS: With a partner or in small groups, discuss the answers to the following questions. You may want to write your answers on a separate sheet of paper to refer to later.

Biotic Potential and Environmental Resistance

1. List some factors that may be part of a species' biotic potential. Identify specific animal or plant species that have these characteristics. (for example, ability to migrate: ducks) (paragraph 5)
2. Which factors of environmental resistance are affecting the giant panda at the present time? What is the overall relationship between biotic potential and environmental resistance for the panda? (paragraph 6 and reading selection in lesson 1)
3. In your own words, state the main idea of this section.

Humankind and Ecosystem Balance

4. In what way is human evolution different from the evolution of other animals? (paragraphs 9–10)
5. Why has this difference led to an imbalance between humankind's biotic potential and environmental resistance? What has been the result of this imbalance? (paragraph 11)
6. Explain the following prediction made in paragraph 12: "There are many indications that the human wave, at least that of humans in a technological society, may be relatively short-lived."
7. Why are ecologists concerned about the *speed* of the changes brought about by technological society? Why does paragraph 14 mention in particular the large number of extinctions? (paragraphs 13–14)
8. How does human reliance on a few animal and plant species make the human ecosystem "inherently unstable"? (paragraph 15)
9. What is meant by "overgrazing"? Why is this phenomenon a problem? (paragraphs 16–17)

10. Paragraph 18 presents the reader with a choice. With your classmates, discuss the nature of this choice. What changes do you feel might need to be made in human society to ensure a more balanced ecosystem?

Becoming a Proficient Writer

Guided Writing: Summarizing an Academic Reading

Summarizing a textbook chapter or other academic selection is both a useful *study* skill and an important *writing* skill. A **summary** is a condensation of the main ideas of a piece of writing. Used for study, its purpose is to highlight main points and concepts with which you should be familiar. Used as part of a longer composition, its purpose is to provide your readers with an objective and accurate account of a piece of writing they have not read.

DIRECTIONS: Write a brief summary of "Ecosystems In and Out of Balance," based on your reading discussion and notes regarding this chapter. Remember that a summary is written in complete sentences and in paragraph form. Following is a process that will help you to write a good summary.

1. Underline main ideas and primary supports in the piece of writing. (You have already done this for this chapter.)
2. On a separate sheet of paper, write down key words and expressions from these points—do *not* write whole sentences from the text, as this will make it more difficult for you to put the author's meaning into your own words.
3. Without looking at your paper, use these key words to say aloud the main ideas of the text as though you were explaining its meaning to another person.
4. Write down these ideas into a paragraph *without* looking back at the original text. Here are some guidelines to keep in mind as you write:
   a. A summary includes the author's main ideas and primary supporting points but does not include secondary supports or details.
   b. Use your own words as much as possible. This is called paraphrasing.
      —Repeat only the key words that do not have accurate synonyms.
      —Try using different grammatical structures.
      —Note: Using the author's words as if they were your own is called plagiarism and must be avoided.
   c. Keep the author's original meaning.
      —Do not take out any ideas that could change the original meaning.
      —Do not add your own opinion.
5. Finally, check your summary with the original text to see if you have included all the necessary points and have expressed them in your own words. Make any necessary changes in your summary.

Comparing Your Summaries

DIRECTIONS: Exchange papers with a partner. Compare your two summaries. Do they include the same points? If not, discuss which points should be included in the summary, which should be omitted, and why. Are both summaries in your own words? If not, how could they be rewritten to paraphrase the author's meaning in other words?

LESSON 3

COMPOSING
ON YOUR OWN

The First Draft

Choosing a Topic

DIRECTIONS: Choose one of the following topics for your essay. Note that each topic requires you to summarize an article on a particular issue or problem and then to develop your opinion about what should be done to solve or alleviate that problem.

A. Write an essay describing the steps you think need to be taken to begin to resolve the problem of ecological imbalance described in the reading for lesson 2. Include in your essay a summary of the chapter "Ecosystems In and Out of Balance" as well as an explanation of what you think should be done to change things. You may want to particularize the topic to your own country by discussing examples of this imbalance in your area and describing what you think the government, business interests, and/or the general public could do to solve the problems. Or you could focus on a particular environmental regulation which you think is unfair or ineffective and then offer an alternative approach.

B. Like the first reading selection on the giant panda, the following short article discusses the threat of extinction facing endangered species. In this case, however, the focus is on the illegal trade in animal products which contributes to this threat. Write an essay which summarizes this article and presents your position on what can be done to solve the problem it describes.

Man Closes In On Wilderness Life
by Robert Ryser

LONDON

Pandas are not the only endangered species. Worldwide trade in wild animals, rare birds, and plants—much of it illegal—also threatens to wipe out thousands of others.

Conservationists warn that within this century "mass extinction" faces about 20 percent of wilderness beings already listed as endangered.

They estimate that legal wildlife trade in everything from parrots to furs has an annual turnover of at least 3 billion dollars. It involves bout 2,400 species of birds and animals and 30,000 plants.

Much of the legal trade is done under license. But there are no controls over the illicit market for products such as rhinoceros horns, elephant tusks, tropical birds and reptile skins.

Some Indonesian and South American parrots go for up to $5,000. Reptiles provide skins for shoes and handbags. Leopards and panthers end up as fur coats. A panda-skin rug is worth $25,000.

Experts cite a sharp decline in elephant herds of Africa, where Third World poverty, economic demand and feeble controls encourage poaching, smuggling and government corruption.

In 1983 alone, more than 80,000 elephants were killed, about 8 percent of the continent's elephant population. Most died to satisfy the demand for ivory tusks by artisans in Japan.

Another African tragedy is the black rhinoceros. Since 1970, its number has fallen from 65,000 to 13,500. One rhino horn, used in Asia as an aphrodisiac and Saudi Arabia for the carved hilts of ceremonial daggers, is worth more than many Africans earn in a year.

Efforts are being made to end such illegal trade, but it is likely to endure as long as the appetite for exotic pets, ivory, fur coats, handbags and other wildlife products is unchecked.

C. Choose a particular ecological problem facing your country or area. This problem may be one mentioned in the readings or it may be a related issue such as air or water pollution. Then, find a relevant article from a magazine or newspaper which discusses this problem or an aspect of it. Write an essay that summarizes your chosen article and presents your opinion on the issue and what should (or should not) be done about it.

D.   Write an essay like the one described in topic C, but in this case choose an issue and an article in your field rather than in the field of ecology.

Generating Ideas

After you've identified the main points of the article you are using for your essay, you'll need to begin generating ideas about the issue(s) raised in that article. In this course you've studied several different techniques for generating ideas. These include brainstorming (individually or in a group), freewriting, looping, and clustering.

DIRECTIONS: Choose two techniques to use in gathering your ideas for this essay. Try the two techniques separately or in combination. Remember that one technique may lay the groundwork for another. For example, a clustering exercise may be used as the basis for a freewriting. Or you may begin with a freewriting to get your mind started in a particular direction and then move to listing or clustering based on what was generated in that freewriting. The choice of techniques and the order in which you use them is entirely up to you. As you begin developing your ideas, you may want to think about several different aspects of the topic. These may include (1) the causes of the problem, (2) its short-term and long-term effects, (3) the steps currently being taken to deal with the problem, (4) additional steps that should be taken (including those on a governmental, community, business, or individual level), and (5) the feasibility of any of the solutions you offer.

Writing the First Draft

Based on your summaries and your own ideas generated about the issue, write a draft of your essay. Be sure to include enough support to convince the reader that your points are valid. You may even want to do some extra research in the library or elsewhere to find additional examples or statistics to include in your support. This would reinforce your ideas and make them more convincing.

Peerediting and Revising

DIRECTIONS: Work with a group of classmates first and then with one other student to peeredit your paper.

1.   Work with your classmates to draw up a list of questions or guidelines to use in evaluating content and development in your partners' papers.
2.   Exchange papers with a classmate. Use the guidelines to comment on both the strengths and the weaknesses of your partner's essay. When you discuss the papers, be sure to point out the strong features as well as to suggest any revisions that may make the paper more effective. After you've discussed each person's draft, return the papers to the writer.
3.   Revise and/or rewrite if necessary.

The Second Draft

Peerediting and Revising

Follow the same peerediting and revising pattern you used for the content of this essay. At this point, your teacher may collect your papers and comment on them.

DIRECTIONS: In unit 8, you and your classmates worked together to develop your own peerediting guidelines to use for that topic. Refer back to those guidelines as a basis for developing a new peerediting framework for the topics in this unit. You might want to consider the following questions.

1. Which of the guidelines refer to general aspects of any successful piece of writing? (questions concerning the introduction, essay focus, adequacy of supporting detail, the conclusion, and so on)

2. Which of the guidelines used in unit 8 would not apply to the topics addressed in this unit?

3. What special features of the essays in this unit should be addressed in the guidelines? (the adequacy of the summary, use of the writer's own words to summarize, the drawing of a clear distinction between the summary and the writer's opinion on the issue, a logical connection between the problem and the proposed solutions, and so on)

Proofreading

When you are satisfied with your revised version of the paper, proofread your final draft for grammatical and mechanical (spelling and punctuation) errors. Use a step-by-step procedure as you've done in previous units.

Sharing Your Writing

DIRECTIONS: If possible, place your seats in a circle to perform this activity.

1. Following the procedure outlined in unit 4, lesson 3 (topic A), pass your paper to the person seated on your left. At the same time, you should receive a paper from the person seated on your right. Read through this paper. You may want to mark any points or sections you particularly like. In addition, on a separate sheet of paper, note any essays which seem especially strong or clear or whose topic might be specific enough and well-developed enough to be used in a letter-to-the-editor column of a local or ecological newspaper. Keep reading and passing papers to the left until your paper is finally returned to you.

2. After the class has read all the papers, identify the ones you felt were particularly strong. What aspects of these essays made them stand out from the rest? Did they include showing details? Were their explanations of the solutions particularly clear? Did their introductions pull you into the topic they were discussing?

3. Choose one or two of the essays which you feel could be written as a letter-to-the-editor. Who would be the audience for such a letter? How would the essay have to be changed to address this audience and to conform to the form and style of a letter-to-the-editor? You may want to form into small groups to draft these letters. Where possible and appropriate, you may even decide to send the letters to a local, national, or international English language newspaper.

Keeping a Journal

1. The reading selection in lesson 2 discusses the general problem of ecological imbalance, but this *general* problem is of course also reflected in many *particular* ways in our daily lives. Look around you at your home, your school, or your locality. Can you detect any evidence of this ecological imbalance? In a journal entry describe this imbalance as you experience it or witness it in your daily life.

2. Often we talk about what the government or society must do to preserve the environment. Are there also changes which an individual can and should make in his or her lifestyle to help accomplish this same goal? Consider your own lifestyle: Are there ways in which you contribute to ecological problems unnecessarily? Are there changes you might make in your habits or activities which would lessen this contribution? Write a journal entry discussing this aspect of your personal lifestyle.

UNIT TEN

ANTICIPATING TOMORROW: THE FUTURE

About This Unit

Throughout this course you have been reading and writing about change—change in your field of work, change in our knowledge of the world, change in human behavior and relationships. As you have progressed through the units of this book, you have also had the opportunity to *experience* change—in this case, change in your own skill level as you have taken on more and more responsibility for comprehending the reading selections and for defining and creating your own writing tasks. Despite your improvement, however, your responsibility has still remained only partial; for in each unit we have continued to provide you with not only the framework and guidelines for your work, but also the specific topics as well. In unit 10, that pattern will finally be broken.

The first difference you may notice about this unit is that it does not have a narrowly defined field as its focus. Instead, we look at the issues of change and the future in a broader perspective and leave it to you to define the specific area of change you would like to explore further. Second, the structure of this unit also differs from that of previous ones. For instance, both reading selections occur in the first lesson; the second lesson is then devoted to writing your composition, and the third lesson to sharing your work. Finally, the main difference between this and previous units is that we have turned the responsibility for all reading and writing tasks over to you. Thus, although we suggest a few discussion questions in lesson 1, you will need to practice the reading skills you have learned throughout the text to comprehend and interpret the reading selections. Also, in lesson 2 you will have the opportunity to compose an essay completely on your own—from the choice of a topic to the final proofreading correction. We will provide you with some *suggested* steps to follow, but the content of your composition is entirely up to you. In lesson 3, you will get a chance to share your ideas and to see how far you and your classmates have come in developing your writing skills.

LESSON 1

THE COSMIC CALENDAR AND CREATIVITY...

About the Selections:

Computerized telecommunications, multinational corporations, manned space flights, mushrooming cities—these are all changes society has undergone in recent decades. Graduation, marriage, a new job, the birth of a child—these are changes an individual might experience in his or her lifetime. But what about the changes that occur very slowly over hundreds, thousands, even millions of years? In the first reading selection, "The Cosmic Calendar," Carl Sagan takes us beyond our own century, even beyond the realm of human experience, to broaden our understanding of change and of time itself. To do this, he has compressed the entire history of the universe, some 15 billion years, into the span of a single "year" in his cosmic calendar. His method might be compared to that of a map maker, who condenses 100 or 1,000 kilometers into each centimeter on the scale of a map. In Sagan's case, the scale is not one of distance, but of time as each second of his cosmic calendar represents 475 real Earth years. Thus, momentous events like the Bronze Age, the Ch'in Dynasty, or the European Crusades become mere seconds or milliseconds in length. As you read this first selection, consider how Sagan's calendar might alter our perspective on the more immediate and short-term changes we have discussed in this course.

Then, in the second selection, "Creativity...", by Isaac Asimov, we return to a more limited time perspective and to the topic with which we began this text—the changing nature of work and what it means for our future. Because work is central to all aspects of human society, however, Asimov looks beyond the future job market to create a broader picture of the life and society that await us in the coming century. As you read this selection, compare Asimov's perspective on work with that of the first readings in this book. Also, consider his comments on other aspects of human endeavor—how do they compare with the readings and perspectives in previous units and with your own experience and expectations?

After you have read the articles, discuss the questions on pages 240 and 241 with your classmates. These may provide a framework for looking at the issue of change in your final compositions.

Before You Read

The two selections presented here are intended to spark your thoughts about change. Both readings contain some sophisticated vocabulary and sentence structure. You may want to read each twice, but don't worry about understanding every detail. Use the boldface sentences in Asimov's article to help you understand the main ideas. Use the footnotes and your context skills to help you interpret the vocabulary.

THE COSMIC CALENDAR
By Carl Sagan

1   The world is very old, and human beings are very young. Significant events in our personal lives are measured in years or less; our lifetimes in decades; our family genealogies[1] in centuries; and all of recorded history in millennia.[2] But we have been preceded by an awesome[3] vista of time, extending for prodigious[4] periods into the past, about which we know little—both because there are no written records and because we have real difficulty in grasping[5] the immensity[6] of the intervals[7] involved.

2   Yet we are able to date events in the remote past. Geological stratification[8] and radioactive dating[9] provide information on archaeological,[10] paleontological[11] and geological events; and astrophysical[12] theory provides data on the ages of planetary surfaces, stars, and the Milky Way Galaxy, as well as an estimate of the time that has elapsed[13] since that extraordinary

[1]**genealogies:** records of ancestry
[2]**millennia:** thousands of years
[3]**awesome:** giving the feeling of wonder and dread
[4]**prodigious:** enormous
[5]**grasping:** understanding
[6]**immensity:** vastness
[7]**intervals:** periods of time
[8]**geological stratification:** method used to date remote events by studying the layers of matter making up the earth's crust
[9]**radioactive dating:** method used to date remote events by studying the decomposition process of various matter
[10]**archaeological:** relating to the study of evidence of human life and culture in the past
[11]**paleontological:** relating to the study of fossils and ancient life form
[12]**astrophysical:** relating to the physics of the stars
[13]**elapsed:** passed

event called the Big Bang—an explosion that involved all of the matter and energy in the present universe. The Big Bang may be the beginning of the universe, or it may be a discontinuity in which information about the earlier history of the universe was destroyed. But it is certainly the earliest event about which we have any record.

3   The most instructive way I know to express this cosmic chronology is to imagine the fifteen-billion-year lifetime of the universe (or at least its present incarnation[14] since the Big Bang) compressed into the span of a single year. Then every billion years of Earth's history would correspond to about twenty-four days of our cosmic year, and one second of that year to 475 real revolutions of Earth about the sun. I present the cosmic chronology in three forms: a list of some representative pre-December dates; a calendar for the

PRE-DECEMBER DATES

Big Bang	January 1
Origin of the Milky Way Galaxy	May 1
Origin of the solar system	September 9
Formation of the Earth	September 14
Origin of life on Earth	~September 25
Formation of the oldest rocks known on Earth	October 2
Date of oldest fossils (bacteria and blue-green algae)	October 9
Invention of sex (by microorganisms)	~November 1
Oldest fossil photosynthetic plants	November 12
Eukaryotes (first cells with nuclei) flourish	November 15

~ = approximately

month of December (see page 236); and a closer look at the late evening of New Year's Eve. On this scale, the events of our history books—even books that make significant efforts to deprovincialize[15] the present— are so compressed that it is necessary to give a second-by-second recounting of the last seconds of the cosmic year. Even then, we find events listed as contemporary that we have been taught to consider as widely separated in time. In the history of life, an

DECEMBER 31

Origin of Proconsul and Ramapithecus, probable ancestors of apes and men	~1:30 P.M.
First humans	~10:30 P.M.
Widespread use of stone tools	11:00 P.M.
Domestication of fire by Peking man	11:46 P.M.
Beginning of most recent glacial period	11:56 P.M.
Seafarers settle Australia	11:58 P.M.
Extensive cave painting in Europe	11:59 P.M.
Invention of agriculture	11:59:20 P.M.
Neolithic civilization; first cities	11:59:35 P.M.
First dynasties in Sumer, Ebla and Egypt; development of astronomy	11:59:50 P.M.
Invention of the alphabet; Akkadian Empire	11:59:51 P.M.
Hammurabic legal codes in Babylon; Middle Kingdom in Egypt	11:59:52 P.M.
Bronze metallurgy; Mycenaean culture; Trojan War; Olmec culture: invention of the compass	11:59:53 P.M.
Iron metallurgy; First Assyrian Empire; Kingdom of Israel; founding of Carthage by Phoenicia	11:59:54 P.M.
Asokan India; Ch'in Dynasty China; Periclean Athens; birth of Buddha	11:59:55 P.M.
Euclidean geometry; Archimedean physics; Ptolemaic astronomy; Roman Empire; birth of Christ	11:59:56 P.M.
Zero and decimals invented in Indian arithmetic; Rome falls; Moslem conquests	11:59:57 P.M.
Mayan civilization; Sung Dynasty China; Byzantine empire; Mongol invasion; Crusades	11:59:58 P.M.
Renaissance in Europe; voyages of discovery from Europe and from Ming Dynasty China; emergence of the experimental method in science	11:59:59 P.M.
Widespread development of science and technology; emergence of a global culture; acquisition of the means for self-destruction of the human species; first steps in spacecraft planetary exploration and the search for extraterrestrial intelligence	Now: The first second of New Year's Day

equally rich tapestry must have been woven in other periods—for example, between 10:02 and 10:03 on the morning of April 6th or September 16th. But we have detailed records only for the very end of the cosmic year.

[14]**incarnation:** form

[15]**deprovincialize:** remove the narrow perspective

COSMIC CALENDAR
DECEMBER

SUNDAY	MONDAY	TUESDAY	WEDNESDAY	THURSDAY	FRIDAY	SATURDAY
	1 Significant oxygen atmosphere begins to develop on Earth.	**2**	**3**	**4**	**5** Extensive vulcanism and channel formation on Mars.	**6**
7	**8**	**9**	**10**	**11**	**12**	**13**
14	**15**	**16** First worms.	**17** Precambrian ends. Paleozoic Era and Cambrian Period begin. Invertebrates flourish.	**18** First oceanic plankton. Trilobites flourish.	**19** Ordovician Period. First fish, first vertebrates.	**20** Silurian Period. First vascular plants. Plants began colonization of land.
21 Devonian Period begins. First insects. Animals begin colonization of land.	**22** First amphibians. First winged insects.	**23** Carboniferous Period. First trees. First reptiles.	**24** Permian Period begins. First dinosaurs.	**25** Paleozoic Era ends. Mesozoic Era begins.	**26** Triassic Period. First mammals.	**27** Jurassic Period. First birds.
28 Cretaceous Period. First flowers. Dinosaurs become extinct.	**29** Mesozoic Era ends. Cenozoic Era and Tertiary Period begin. First cetaceans. First primates.	**30** Early evolution of frontal lobes in the brains of primates. First hominids. Giant mammals flourish.	**31** End of the Pliocene Period. Quatenary (Pleistocene and Holocene) Period. First humans.			

The chronology corresponds to the best evidence now available. But some of it is rather shaky. No one would be astounded[16] if, for example, it turns out that plants colonized the land in the Ordovician rather than the Silurian Period; or that segmented worms appeared earlier in the Precambrian Period than indicated. Also, in the chronology of the last ten seconds of the cosmic year, it was obviously impossible for me to include all significant events: I hope I may be excused for not having explicitly[17] mentioned advances in art, music and literature or the historically significant American, French, Russian and Chinese revolutions.

The construction of such tables and calendars is inevitably[18] humbling. It is disconcerting[19] to find that in such a cosmic year the Earth does not condense out of

---

[16]**astounded:** greatly surprised
[17]**explicitly:** specifically and directly
[18]**inevitably:** unavoidably
[19]**disconcerting:** upsetting

interstellar[20] matter until early September; dinosaurs emerge on Christmas Eve; flowers arise on December 28th; and men and women originate at 10:30 P.M. on New Year's Eve. All of recorded history occupies the last ten seconds of December 31; and the time from the waning[21] of the Middle Ages to the present occupies little more than one second. But because I have arranged it that way, the first cosmic year has just ended. And despite the insignificance of the instant we have so far occupied in cosmic time, it is clear that what happens on and near Earth at the beginning of the second cosmic year will depend very much on the scientific wisdom and distinctly human sensitivity of mankind.

[20]**interstellar:** between the stars
[21]**waning:** declining

CREATIVITY WILL DOMINATE OUR TIME AFTER THE CONCEPTS OF WORK AND FUN HAVE BEEN BLURRED BY TECHNOLOGY
by Isaac Asimov

1   **Periodically in history, there come periods of great transition in which work changes its meaning.** There was a time, perhaps 10,000 years ago, when human beings stopped feeding themselves by hunting game and gathering plants, and increasingly turned to agriculture. In a way, that represented the invention of "work," the hard daily labor designed to ensure food and the wherewithal[1] of life.

2   Then, in the latter decades of the 18th century, as the Industrial Revolution began in Great Britain, there was another transition in which the symbols of work were no longer the hoe and the plow; they were replaced by the mill and the assembly line. The aristrocrat no longer cultivated[2] a pale skin as his mark that he did not have to go out into the fields to labor; instead, he cultivated a deep tan to show that he did not have to stay indoors to labor.

3   **And now we stand at the brink of a change that will be the greatest of all, for work in its old sense will disappear altogether.** To most people, work has always been an effortful exercising of mind or body—compelled[3] by the bitter necessity of earning the necessities of life—plus an occasional period of leisure in which to rest or have fun.

4   People have always tried desperately to foist off[4] work on others: on human slaves, serfs or peasants; on hired hands, on animals, on ingenious machines. With the Industrial Revolution, machinery—powered first by steam, then by electricity and internal combustion engines—took over the hard physical tasks and relieved the strain on human and animal muscles.

5   There remained, however, the "easier" labor that did not require muscle, and that machines, however, ingenious,

[1]**wherewithal:** necessities
[2]**cultivate:** develop; grow
[3]**compel:** *(v)*/**compulsion** *(n)*: force
[4]**foist off:** (work): make someone else do the work

could not do—the labor that required the human eyes, ears, judgment and mind. If this work did not require huge effort, muscles and sweat, it nevertheless had its miseries, for it tended to be dull, repetitious, and boring. Whether one works over a sewing machine, an assembly line or a typewriter, day after day, there is always the sour sense of endlessly doing something unpleasant under compulsion, something that stultifies[5] one's mind and wastes one's life.

6   And yet, such jobs have been characteristic of the human condition in the first three-quarters of the 20th century. They've made too little demand on the human mind and spirit to keep them fresh and alive, made too much demand for any machine to serve the purpose—until now.

7   **The electronic computer, invented in the 1940's and improved at breakneck speed, was a machine that, for the first time, seemed capable of doing work that had until until then been the preserve of the human mind.** With the coming of the microchip in the 1970's, computers became compact enough, versatile[6] enough and (most important of all) cheap enough to serve as the brains of affordable machines that could take their place on the assembly line and in the office.

8   This means that the dull, the boring, the repetitious, the mind-stultifying work will begin to disappear from the job market—is *already* beginning to disappear. This of course, will introduce two vital sets of problems—is *already* introducing them.

9   First, what will happen to the human beings who have been working at these disappearing jobs?

10   Second, where will we get the human beings that will do the new jobs that will appear—jobs that are demanding, interesting and mind-exercising, but that require a high-tech level of thought and education?

11   **Clearly there will be a painful period of transition, one that is starting already, and one that will be in full swing[7] as the 21st century begins.**

12   The first problem, that of technological unemployment, will be temporary, for it will arise out of the fact that there is now a generation of employees who have not been educated to fit the computer age. However, (in advanced nations, at least) they will be the last generation to be so lacking, so that with them this problem will disappear—or, at least, diminish[8] to the point of non-crisis proportions.

13   The second problem—that of developing a large enough number of high-tech minds to run a high-tech world—will be no problem at all, once we adjust our thinking.

14   In the first place, the computer age will introduce a total revolution in our notions[9] of education, and is beginning to do so now.... The coming of the computer will make learning fun, and a successfully stimulated mind will learn quickly. It will undoubtedly turn out that the "average" child is much more intelligent and creative than we generally suppose. There was a time, after all, when the ability to read and write was confined to a very small group of "scholars" and almost all of them would have scouted[10] the notion that just about anyone could learn the intricacies[11] of literacy. Yet with mass education general literacy came to be a fact.

15   Right now, creativity seems to be con-

---

[5]**stultify:** to make foolish or ineffective
[6]**versatile:** able to be used in many ways
[7]**in full swing:** fully under way; at its highest level
[8]**diminish:** lessen; become smaller
[9]**notion:** idea
[10]**scouted:** rejected; scorned
[11]**intricacies:** complexities

fined to a very few, and it is easy to suppose that that is the way it must be. However, with the proper availability of computerized education, humanity will surprise the elite[12] few once again.

16   Granted, now that the problems of unemployment and education will be on the way toward solution, what kind of work will there be aside from what is involved in that solution?

17   **For one thing, much of human effort that is today put into "running the world" will be unnecessary.** With computers, robots and automation, a great deal of the daily grind will appear to be running itself. This is nothing startling. It is a trend that has been rapidly on its way ever since World War II.

18   The result of this trend will be that more and more working people will have more and more leisure. That is also not startling, for we have been witnessing the steady increase in leisure for a long time. This means that more and more "work" will involve the filling of this leisure time. Show business and sports will grow steadily more important. (A comment I once made, which has been frequently quoted is: "One third of the world will labor to amuse the other two thirds.")

19   And what of the work that is more easily recognized as work in the traditional sense?

20   **There will still be much that is peculiarly human and will not be computerized except at the fringes[13]** (I use a word processor, which makes the mechanics of my work a bit easier, but the thing steadfastly refuses to write my essays for me. I still have to sit here, thinking.) In other words, those who are involved in literature, music, and the arts will be busier than ever in the leisure society, since their audience will grow steadily greater.

21   There will also be enormous changes. In business, the accent will be on decision-making, on administration. Offices and factories will be "black boxes" in which the routine details will run themselves, but in which men and women will handle the controls.

22   Nor will this have to be done on the spot. We will be living in an "information society" in which we will not have to transfer mass to transfer information. We won't have to send human beings from A to B in order that their mouth may give directions.

23   With computerization knitting the world into a tight unit, and with the work of directing operations and gathering information easily done from anywhere, the world will begin to decentralize. There will be an increasing tendency for cities to dwindle[14] (this is already a recognized trend, at least in the United States).

24   **It may sound as though the 21st century, with its increasing leisure, its black-box offices and factories, its emphasis on long-distance work from the home, may become a kind of society that will be too secure, too easy.**

    Not so!

25   We will also be entering the Space Age with a vengeance;[15] and perhaps the most important type of work facing us as the new century opens will be that which is involved in gaining command of the resources of space.

26   We will be building solar power stations that will absorb the full range of sunlight in space and turn it into microwaves that will be beamed to Earth. We will be building observatories to study the universe away from the interference of Earth's

---

[12]**elite:** the best, most powerful, or most intelligent people in a group

[13]**fringes:** edges; the least central or important part of something

[14]**dwindle:** to become smaller and smaller

[15]**with a vengeance:** in an extreme or forceful way

atmosphere and of human-made light and radio beams. We will be building laboratories to study the uses of space's unusual properties—high and low temperature, hard radiation, zero gravity.

27   We will be building factories that will be turning out products making use of these properties, products that could be turned out only with difficulty, if at all, on Earth's surfaces. We will be building mining stations on the Moon to get the material out of which all these structures will be built, and space settlements on which the men and women working on all these projects can live and on which they can build families and new societies.

28   And for every person in space engaged in these magnificent new goals, there will be a dozen people on Earth supporting the ventures.

29   In the beginning decades of the 21st century, with the aid of computers and robots, all the future of humanity will be coming to fruition[16] in the emptiness we will be filling, and there will be incredible excitement and precious little boredom in that.

30   In fact, the 21st century, for all its advancement, will be one of the great pioneering periods of human history, as people work under totally new conditions, doing totally new things in totally new ways, taking totally new risks to achieve totally new triumphs.

[16]**fruition:** fulfillment; good results

"Creativity will dominate our time after the concepts of work and fun have been blurred by technology" by Isaac Asimov, *Personnel Administrator*, December 1983. Copyright © 1984 American Society for Personnel Administration. Reprinted by permission of Isaac Asimov.

After You Read: Responding to Reading

The two articles you have just read are both quite thought-provoking. Carl Sagan looks back in time, relating it to our universe and the events we consider to be significant. Isaac Asimov looks ahead as he presents his view of the future. The following questions will give you a chance to examine further some of the stimulating and fascinating issues that these articles raise. Your teacher will help you to decide which of these questions you will address in class.

About ''The Cosmic Calendar''

1. What historical events do you consider to be significant? Do they assume less importance when you consider them with Sagan's time perspective in mind? Why or why not?

2. In paragraph 4 Sagan apologies for not being able to include all ''significant'' events in the last ten seconds of the cosmic year.

    a. In your opinion, did he overlook significant events that you believe he should have included? What are they and why are they as important as the events that he did include?

    b. Did he include events that you believe are not important enough to mention? Why?

3. Sagan begins the last paragraph of the article by saying that the Cosmic Calendar's perspective of time is humbling. What do you think he means by this statement? Do you agree with him? Why or why not?

4. "And despite the insignificance of the instant we have so far occupied in cosmic time, it is clear that what happens on and near Earth at the beginning of the second cosmic year will depend very much on the scientific wisdom and the distinctly human sensitivity of mankind." What is the meaning of Sagan's concluding sentence of the article? Do you agree with it? With your classmates, exchange views of humankind's role in a vast and infinite universe. Then relate this last sentence to the issues raised in the second reading of unit 9, "Ecosystems In and Out of Balance."

About "Creativity..."

1. Discuss your society's attitudes about work. Is work revered? Does your society have a history of "foisting off work"? What is your personal attitude about work? Has it been influenced by the attitude of your society?

2. Your textbook addresses the following as unit themes:

Sociology/Occupation (unit 1)	Athletics (unit 4) Business (unit 5)	Music/Physiology (unit 7)
Demography (unit 2)	Anthropology	Psychology (unit 8)
Astronomy (unit 3)	(unit 6)	Ecology (unit 9)

In his article, Asimov makes reference, either directly or indirectly, to many of these topics. Find any reference made to these in the article. Then comment on Asimov's view of each topic he mentions. Is his perspective the same as the perspective presented in the readings from earlier units?

3. How does Asimov view the role of creativity in the future? Compare your vision of the role of creativity in the twenty-first century to Asimov's.

4. In the first unit of this book you considered your occupation as it relates to the future. In this article, Asimov introduces his own ideas about work in the years to come. Does Asimov address your kind of work in the article? Do you agree with his vision of the future of your occupation? Why or why not?

Lesson 2

Composing on Your Own

The First Draft

Generating Ideas

• Defining Your Topic

Defining a topic is one of the most challenging and most important aspects of good writing. The first step obviously is to find a general area of interest that you would like to pursue further—in this case an area that involves or reflects some kind of change. Then you will need to narrow down that area in order to focus your writing on a well-defined point or message, considering both your audience and purpose as you do so.

DIRECTIONS: Establish the topic you wish to write about by following these steps.

Step 1: Reading and Thinking

    a. With the concept of *change* in mind, read back over the entries in your freewriting notebook and journal.

    b. Glance through any reading selections you particularly liked and note specific points that interested you. You might also want to consider your answers to the discussion questions in lesson 1 of this unit as well as any changes you've seen in your own field of work or study.

c.   As you read and think about the concept of change, identify three areas of interest to you.

Step 2: Freewriting

Freewrite on each of your areas of interest. After you have finished each freewriting, write one or two loops (focused freewritings) about specific points that you might want to concentrate on.* *Note:* Your purpose in this looping exercise is to see if you have enough interest in a particular issue or enough to say about it for it to become the topic of your paper.

Step 3: Working In a Group

Form a group with three of your classmates. (The other members of your group do not have to be working on the same topic as you; in fact, it will probably be more interesting if you are working on different topics.) Each group member should then take a turn presenting his or her areas of interest and the possible essay topics for the other members to respond to and discuss.

For example, if you are the first student to begin the discussion, tell the group about the topic area that interests you the most and about the possibilities for your focused topic. If you are unsure of your specific topic, your classmates might help you with a group brainstorming session. Be sure to listen closely to your classmates' suggestions, for one of the points they mention may turn out to be the very one that sparks your interest. When the first student has finished discussing one area of interest, the next person in the group should present an area and topics he or she would like to pursue. Continue taking turns presenting and discussing topics in this manner until you have all identified a *specific* topic of interest. If any group members have not chosen a topic after the first round of presentations, they should take another turn to explore a different area of interest. Remember, when you are giving feedback to your classmates, think about topics that would be likely to interest the potential *reader* of the essay as well as the writer.

Step 4: Determining Your Message

Now that you have chosen your topic, what will you say about it?

a.   Think about your potential audience and about your purpose for writing to that audience. Are you trying to supply your readers with information they might not otherwise have? Are you trying to help them accomplish a particular task? Or perhaps you want to convince them that a certain action is necessary. You will need to define both your audience and your purpose before you can determine exactly what message you wish to communicate to your reader.

For example, if you are particularly interested in the issue of stress, your topic may concern stress in an academic situation, or even more specifically, stress related to an important examination. If your audience consists of fellow students, then your purpose may be to suggest ways that they can cope better with that stress. If, on the other hand,

---

*See unit 2, lesson 1, for a discussion of looping.

your audience is the faculty or examiners responsible for the test, your purpose may be to convince them that placing too much pressure on students can be counterproductive, and you may want to propose ways in which the pre- and postexamination stress may be reduced for better test results.

Thus, the choice of your audience and purpose may greatly affect the content of your paper; that is, the message that you communicate is largely determined by who you want to read the paper and why you want them to read it.

b. Once you have decided on your audience and purpose, develop your topic—your message—into a statement. Like a thesis statement, this sentence will guide the development of your essay. The exact wording of the statement may change, of course, as you write your composition. Your ideas about your topic may also change, so don't feel that what you write now will have to be what appears in your final essay as the thesis statement. For that reason, let's call this a *guiding* statement, rather than a thesis statement.

Step 5: Evaluating Your Guiding Statements

DIRECTIONS: Again, form into small groups.

a. Discuss the guiding statement prepared by each student. If any of you are having trouble forming a statement, ask for advice from your classmates.

b. Then, each group should choose one or two statements that seem to create the most interest in the group.

c. Write these statements on the board for the class to discuss.

d. Read over the statements on the board, and as a class consider the following questions:

—Which of the statements have well-focused topics?

—Which of the statements have a clear message?

—Which of the statements and topics do you find the most interesting? Why?

—Based on your answers to these questions, decide which two sentences are the best examples of clear, interesting guiding statements. Discuss the probable audience and purpose of each statement. Then discuss how you might support each of these statements in an essay. (For example, would you use statistics about the number of students who become ill or suicidal while studying for the examination? Would you use quotes from famous psychologists about how stress prevents learning? Would you use your own experience to suggest ways to cope with the stress?)

e. Now return to your groups and again share your guiding statements. This time, evaluate each one based on the criteria which developed from the class discussion. How could the writer make the focus or the message of the statement clearer? Will the topic be interesting to the reader? What type of evidence could be used to support the author's message?

● Developing Your Topic

Now that you have your topic defined and you have begun thinking about ways to support it, you are ready to develop your ideas and plan your essay. One possible way to do this is to use the cluster technique you learned in unit 8. If you decide to use this method, you may want to follow the procedure described next. *Note:* This is only one possible method of many. Choose the method(s) that work best for you.

DIRECTIONS: Use the following steps to expand your ideas. Form a group to do Step 3.

Step 1: Clustering

    a. Start by writing your topic in the center of a sheet of paper.

    b. Then, around the topic jot down any points you could use to support your message.

    c. Draw a line from each point to your topic.

    d. Next, develop more specific clusters around relevant points you wish to develop further.

    e. Continue in this manner until you have written all the points that come to mind on your topic. An example cluster on examination stress appears on page 246.

Step 2: Expanding Your Cluster

    a. Which of the supporting points are more relevant to your audience and your message?

    b. What evidence could you use to develop each point? Add this information to the cluster.

    c. Are you already familiar with the evidence you plan to use? If so, you may want to freewrite to begin developing that evidence. If not, you'll need to plan how you can obtain the evidence you need. (For example, to get statistics on the frequency of suicides associated with important exams, you would probably have to use your school or city library.)

    d. How could you introduce the topic to spark your readers' interest?

Step 3: Working in a Group

    a. Are the supporting points logically related to the main point the student is trying to make and are they relevant to the audience? Are there other points the student hasn't considered?

    b. Is the type of evidence the student has chosen appropriate for the message, purpose, and audience? Can you suggest other evidence the student might consider?

    c. Is the proposed introduction interesting? Can you suggest alternative ways to begin the essay?

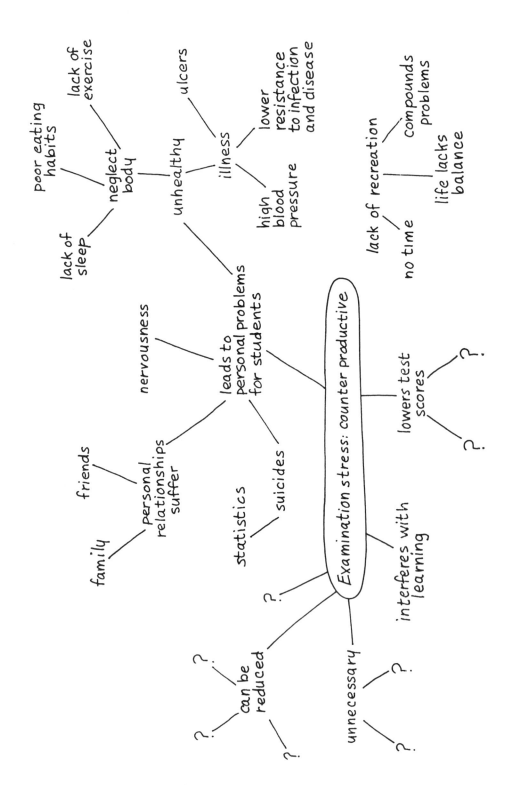

Examination stress: counter productive

leads to personal problems for students

neglect body
- poor eating habits
- lack of exercise
- lack of sleep

unhealthy
- illness
  - ulcers
  - lower resistance to infection and disease
  - high blood pressure

lack of recreation
- no time
- life lacks balance
  - compounds problems

nervousness

personal relationships suffer
- friends
- family

suicides
- statistics
- ?

lowers test scores
- ?
- ?

can be reduced
- ?
- ?
- ?

interferes with learning

unnecessary
- ?
- ?

Based on the ideas you receive from your classmates, modify or expand your plan as needed. Again, you may want to do more freewriting or brainstorming to develop your ideas further.

Writing the First Draft and Peerediting

Now you are ready to write your essay.

DIRECTIONS: After writing your essay and analyzing it, work with a classmate to reconsider your draft.

1. Prepare a draft of your paper which you will share with one of your classmates.
2. Construct a flowchart of your draft essay (see unit 5 for a review of flowcharts). Bring both the draft and the flowchart with you to class.
3. Exchange papers (but not flowcharts) with a partner. Read through your partner's essay; mark or jot down any points you want to discuss later.
4. Discuss each essay. With the peerediting-for-content guidelines you have been using, decide on the necessary changes for each paper. Remember that this is just a first draft. Your focus should be on the main supporting points and the adequacy and relevance of the evidence relating to the audience and purpose. You will edit the papers more thoroughly in the second draft stage.

The Second Draft

Peerediting

DIRECTIONS: After revising on your own, exchange ideas with a partner about each other's paper.

1. Exchange papers again with the same partner.
2. After you have reread your partner's paper, construct a flowchart of the composition as you understand it.
3. Return your partner's paper and receive yours back.
4. Compare the flowchart you made for your own composition with the one your partner made for it.
    a. Are they the same? If not, how are they different?
    b. Do the differences indicate that the relationship of your ideas was unclear? If so, how could they be made clearer?
    c. Do the flowcharts indicate any areas that need further development or reorganization?
    d. Discuss any changes that seem appropriate.

Writing the Second Draft

Based on the discussion with your partner, write a second draft of your paper. Be sure to make any needed changes in organization and support. In addition, focus this time on your introduction and conclusion.

1. Will they be interesting to your readers?
2. Do they introduce and wrap up the topic and the essay sufficiently?
3. Are they linked to the body of your paper with clear transitions and paragraph hooks?
4. Are there clear transitions and paragraph hooks throughout the essay?

Peerediting and Revising/Rewriting

Exchange revised drafts with a partner. Using the peerediting guidelines you developed in units 8 and 9, read and comment on your partner's paper.

Note: Before you begin, you may want to call your partner's attention to particular aspects or parts of your essay that you would like your partner to focus on. For example, if you have been working especially hard to improve your use of transitions and paragraph hooks, you might as your partner to pay special attention to these features in your paper. Also, as you read your partner's composition, be sure to note aspects of the paper that you particularly liked, and jot down any additional comments you want to stress in your discussion. After you have finished reading, discuss both the strengths and weaknesses of each paper.

Based on your partner's comments, prepare the final draft of your essay.

Proofreading

At this point, you are ready for the last step in your writing process: proofreading your final draft.

DIRECTIONS: Approach the final step of the process with the knowledge and skill you have acquired. Take enough time for this final step.

1. Read through your paper for intuitive knowledge.
2. Then, look for one type of error at a time. You may want to check for subject-verb agreement, verb tense, word endings, punctuation, and spelling, Focus, above all, on the kinds of problems you have been working on in your past essays.

    Use the technique or techniques that you have found most helpful in the past (reading the paper aloud exactly as it is written; beginning with the last sentence of the paper and reading backwards, a sentence at a time, and so forth).
3. When you are satisfied with your essay, turn it in to your teacher.

LESSON 3

SHARING YOUR WRITING

Throughout this text, you have shared, in one way or another, each of the compositions that you have written. For this final assignment, we offer several different possibilities for sharing your work. For all of the following suggestions, keep in mind that you will be asked to comment on your classmates' papers. Therefore, consider taking notes on what you hear and/or read so that you do not forget your first reactions to the piece.

DIRECTIONS: With your classmates and your teacher, choose one of the following suggestions to share your final composition.

1. Do a read-around as a full class or in a small group.
2. Read your paper aloud to the class as a whole or to a small group.
3. Orally present the ideas you have written about in your composition. (Your teacher can help you with ideas about oral presentations.)

Whatever method you use to share your work, the class or group should respond to the *ideas* you have presented. Remember that the reason we write is **to communicate a message to an audience.** When we see that we have successfully shared our thoughts with our readers, we enjoy a sense of accomplishment at having achieved our goal.

INDEX

AUTHOR INDEX